Discovering Acts

DISCOVERING ACTS

The Guideposts
Home Bible Study Program

GUIDEPOSTS

Carmel   New York 10512

The Scripture quotation contained on page 119 is from the Revised Standard Version of the Bible, copyright © 1946 (renewed 1973), 1955 (renewed 1980), 1971 by the Division of Christian Education of the National Council of the Churches of Christ in the U.S.A., and used by permission. All rights reserved.

The photographs on the pages listed below are reproduced by permission of the following photographers and organizations:

The Bettmann Archive: 92 and 151
Leo De Wys: 20/Van Phillips; 67/Van Phillips; 93/Vanderwall; 96/H. Byram
Intl. Stock Photo: 57 and 133/Ira Lipsky
Photo Researchers: 55/Porterfield Chickering; 82/Brian Blake; 86/Porterfield
    Chickering; 87/G. Tomsich; 131/Porterfield Chickering
Floyd W. Thatcher: 89, 98, 99, 106, 109, 112, 153
Gerald Ring: 94

THE GUIDEPOSTS HOME BIBLE STUDY PROGRAM
The Acts of the Apostles:
    1. DISCOVERING ACTS
    2. My Working Bible
    3. My Journal of Acts
    4. Knowing More About Acts

All Scripture verses referenced herein are from the King James Version of the Bible.

Designed by Elizabeth Woll.

Printed in the United States of America.

Contents

How to Use
the Guideposts Home
Bible Study Program

1. Read the passages in your *Working Bible* that are included in the appropriate lesson material in *Discovering Acts*. For example, to study Lesson one, read Acts 1:1–2:4. In the margins of your *Working Bible* jot down any notes you'd like to call special attention to.
2. Then, to amplify the Scriptures you've read, study Lesson one in *Discovering Acts*. As you read the lesson keep your *Working Bible* open so you can look up the many Scripture references that are included in the lesson.
3. When you complete each lesson, quiz yourself on what you've learned, with the quiz booklet, *Knowing More About Acts*.
4. When you have your devotions, turn to the appropriate lesson in your *Journal of Acts*.

   Repeat this "rhythm" as you read each lesson, to get the most from your study of God's Word.

Publisher's Introduction

To study the book of Acts is to participate in an adventure of faith which began in Jerusalem and ended some thirty years later in Rome, which was the capital of a vast empire that stretched from Britain to Arabia.

The characters in this drama include provincial governors, Roman centurions and soldiers, kings, common folk, and aristocrats. There is Stephen, the first Christian to die for his faith; an Ethiopian finance officer; James, the Lord's brother and head of the Jerusalem church; Cornelius; Aquila and Priscilla; Silas and Barnabas—an almost endless cast of important characters. But Peter is the main feature in the first part of the story, and Paul is on center stage during the last part. However, throughout the entire story the central figure is always Jesus, the risen Lord.

While not written as history, the book of Acts gives us our only record of the beginnings of Christianity—from Jesus' instructions to His disciples between the resurrection and His ascension, to the coming of the Holy Spirit at Pentecost and the founding of God's new order, the Church. From Jerusalem, empowered believers took the Good News of salvation throughout Judea, Samaria, and Galilee—all of Palestine. And from there we trace its rapid-fire movement to Syrian Antioch, Asia Minor, Greece, and finally to Rome.

Traditionally, Luke has been accepted as the author of

Acts, the second volume to the third Gospel. This gives Luke, the only gentile writer in the New Testament, the distinction of writing more than one-fourth of the New Testament. We are not sure of Luke's beginnings, but tradition suggests that he may have come from either Syrian Antioch or Philippi. We do know that he was a physician, a companion of Paul in many of his travels, and an able writer and historian.

We know, too, that Luke was with Paul on his last trip to Jerusalem, throughout his imprisonment at Caesarea, and on his final journey to Rome. This means that much of Acts is an eyewitness account, and what isn't came to Luke from reliable eyewitnesses.

The time and place where Acts was written cannot be determined for certain. However, tradition seems to favor a date between A.D. 60 and 70. Although there are those who would date the writing as late as the early part of the second century, it is generally conceded that it would not have appeared later than A.D. 90. Tradition also holds that it was written in Rome.

As we move now into this "bridge" book between the Gospels and the Epistles, which follow, we find God at work through His Holy Spirit in the hearts of Jew and gentile alike. We see a vigorous and energized young Church on the move. The mood is one of holy restlessness as first-generation Christians witness to the life-changing power of the gospel of Jesus. His new fellowship is beginning to take shape—nothing could stop it then; nothing can stop it now. *We are the church*, and no evil force can prevail against us.

Preface

Every day millions of people listen to Paul Harvey's broad-cast, "The Rest of the Story." By listening to his creative presentations they can expand their knowledge of well-known people and events. In much the same fashion, the book of Acts is God's "rest of the story." Writing under the inspiration of the Holy Spirit, Luke continues the story he began in his Gospel, with his second volume as he shows us what happened to the Christian faith after Jesus' ascension.

The time period covered by the book of Acts is approxi-mately A.D. 29–67. It was a time of peace and stability in the Roman Empire. Travel was relatively easy and safe. The common language of Greek made communication possible throughout the empire. In short, the time was ripe for the expansion of the Christian community. And that is precisely what the book of Acts describes. It begins with a small band of believers in Jerusalem and ends with Christianity existing all over the known world. In between is a dramatic narrative that reads like a modern-day adven-ture story.

But we should not let the fast-moving quality of the book blind us to the careful piece of history that it is. Luke demonstrates the same care for order and detail in this book that he did in his earlier Gospel account. Many schol-ars agree that the clue for organization can be found in Acts 1:8. Here we see both the centrality of the Holy Spirit and the plan of expansion that can be traced throughout the rest of the book: "...ye shall be witnesses unto me both in Jerusalem, and in all Judea, and in Samaria, and unto the uttermost part of the earth."

Thematically, Acts focuses on the work of the Holy Spirit through the lives of the early disciples. In fact, some scholars have said that the book could have been entitled "The Acts of the Holy Spirit through the Apostles." As we study this book, we will often focus on the idea of effective witnessing, drawing parallels between the first century and ours. In addition, we will come in contact with the basic content of early Christianity through a number of important sermons. And from start to finish we will see how God worked to create Christian community and to establish Christianity as a universal religion.

To get you started, here is an outline of the portions of Acts we will be studying in the next eight lessons:

1. Getting Ready to Go (1:1–2:4)
2. Growing under Pressure (2:5–8:3)
3. Expanding the Territory (8:4–12:25)
4. Establishing the Pattern (13:1–15:35)
5. Responding to the Unexpected: Paul's Second Missionary Journey (15:36–18:22)
6. Strengthening the Fellowship: Paul's Third Missionary Journey 23–20:38)
7. Facing the Enemies (21:1–26:32)
8. Faithful to the End: Paul's Journey to Rome (27:1–28:31)

A knowledge of the message of Acts is essential if we are to understand how Christianity moved from Jesus to Paul—from Palestine to the world. Without it we would not only have a historical "blank," we would also fail to discover many ways in which the Holy Spirit can use us in the continued expansion of the Church.

LESSON 1
ACTS 1:1—2:4

Getting Ready To Go

Thank You for the privilege of learning more about witnessing to my faith through this lesson. AMEN.

Have you ever wanted to practice something before actually deciding whether or not to do it? When I first felt a call into a teaching ministry, I tried to get a job as a teaching assistant so I could give it a try before buckling down to the rigors of doctoral studies. I did not get such a job, and today I'm thankful I didn't, for I had no idea how unprepared I was even to do the work of a teaching assistant. But God knew, and through the leading of circumstances He said, "Steve, I must prepare you before I can use you."

That's where the book of Acts begins. It opens with a group of people whom God intended to use to change the world. But they were not ready yet. They didn't fully realize it, but they needed to be prepared. I believe that's what the fifty days between the resurrection of Jesus and Pentecost were all about. It is easy for us to overlook this needed time of preparation because we are told so little about what happened during those days.

We are told, though, that during the forty days between His resurrection and His ascension, Jesus taught the disciples about "things pertaining to the kingdom of God" (1:3). This must have been the most intensive time of instruction the disciples had ever known. In his Gospel, Luke says that Jesus: "...opened their understanding, that they might understand the scriptures" (24:45). That in itself is amazing, and it speaks of the depth of teaching and learning that took place.

The Main Ingredients of Effective Witnessing (1:1–2)

Luke wastes no time in getting to the heart of what much of this book is about, which is Christian witnessing. In the first two verses we encounter the main ingredients of effective witnessing: the seeker, the servant, and the Saviour. Because they are so important, we will look carefully at each of them right at the beginning. These three elements appear repeatedly throughout the book, and an examination of them will help us gain insights into our own witnessing today.

The Seeker.

Theophilus, the person to whom Luke addressed both his Gospel and the book of Acts, is the seeker. The only clue we get about his relationship to Christianity is found in Luke 1:4, where he is said to have been "instructed" in the faith. This may mean he was a recent convert who was receiving initial training, or it may simply mean that Theophilus had been told some things about the faith and was still trying to make up his mind. Either way, though, he was interested enough to receive two lengthy communications from Luke.

His name may provide a clue. It means "one who loves God." One of the important messages of the book of Acts is that God puts "Theophiluses" (God lovers) in our pathway. They may be outside or inside the church. Our challenge and opportunity is to be sensitive to them and to be willing to give them the time and attention they need to become enriched and whole in the Christian faith.

Even today there are many people outside the church who are searching for God. They are sending loud signals by their involvement in cults and the occult, by their growing despair over the world's problems and our inability to solve them, by their feelings of anxiety and loneliness, and by their deep desires for genuine relationships in a depersonalized world full of "one-night stands." These are all signs that people are open to a relationship with God through Christ, and it is important for us to be sensitive to the "signals" that people around us today are sending.

Then there are Theophiluses within the church fellowship who have a marginal or cursory understanding of and commitment to the Christian faith. These people need to be introduced to the power of personal faith made real by the Holy Spirit. Catherine Marshall once said that many need the "Something More" dimension of Christianity —and it is this "Something More" that comes through loud and clear in Acts. I'm sure we all know people like this, people who just might come alive if they were given special instruction, care, and attention by other believers.

The Servants.

That's where the servants come into the picture. For every Theophilus, there must be at least one Luke. People are won by people. God reached us by becoming human in Jesus Christ. And we reach others by offering them our faith wrapped in our humanity. Christian witnessing is always "incarnational." It began with *the* Incarnation; it continues in the multiplied incarnations of Christ, who lives out His life through those who serve Him.

Who are the servants? The book of Acts supplies the answer. They are the "quiet people"—the servant Christians—most of whose names are not even recorded in Scripture. To be sure there are some major figures and leaders in the drama of Acts, but these are outnumbered a thousand to one by the ordinary followers. The word "celebrity" doesn't exist in God's dictionary, but the word "saint" does. We must forever erase from our minds the notion that only the famous people, the champions, and beauty contest winners are useful to God. This is often the erroneous impression we get in many media ministries. But it is just as false as the pre-Reformation belief that only the priests could rightly read and interpret the Bible. If we fall for the heresy of the "celebrity syndrome," it will take another Christian Reformation to set us right again.

The Saviour.

This brings us to the third ingredient, the Saviour. The only reason we even dare to believe we can influence someone else's life for Christ is because Jesus is real and alive! He continued His ministry through the Holy Spirit after His ascension. Luke's first treatise was only what "Jesus began to do and teach." That's why a second volume was needed. But we must also remember that Christ's ministry did not end with the last page of Acts. It continues today.

There are more Theophiluses in the world right now

than there were when Christ lived on the earth. And there are more Christians alive now than there were when Luke wrote Acts. When we couple that with the knowledge that Christ is just as alive as He ever was, we can know beyond a doubt that our Christian witnessing is meant to be effective. The first two verses of Acts not only remind us of the main ingredients needed then, they also place you and me squarely in the picture of Christian expansion today. Our study of these lessons will be profitable as long as we keep that perspective clearly in mind.

The Master Teacher (1:3–11)

The ultimate purpose of teaching is not just to convey information, but to change people. We've already said that the disciples needed to be changed, to be better prepared for the ministry that would soon be theirs. In Chapter 1:3–11, Luke shows us Jesus' teaching method for accomplishing that change. And it is clear from the rest of Acts that the method was successful. The days between Jesus' resurrection and Pentecost was a time when the Master Teacher got His followers ready for the greatest challenge of their lives. Let's see how He did it.

Jesus Teaches by Revelation.

He concentrated first on *revelation*. Luke says: "...he shewed himself alive ... by many infallible proofs" (1:3). The Greek language used here is quite strong, with each modifying word in "many infallible proofs" reinforcing the others. If we were saying it today, we might put it this way: "Jesus showed himself alive in ways that left *no doubt about it*." This was precisely what the disciples needed. They had to *know* that death had not defeated Jesus. It would never have been enough to be told this. They had to see and experience it.

I remember those days during the Vietnam war when word began to circulate that the POWs would soon be coming home. Lists were released. Families wept at the thought of being reunited with loved ones they hadn't seen for years. But there was also a hesitancy. Were the lists accurate? Would the individuals listed really be coming home? Doubts were not finally erased until wives, children, and relatives saw *their* soldier walking down the steps of the airplane. Sight made the difference!

The old saying is correct: "Seeing *is* believing." Jesus knew that, so He showed himself alive (1:3) in ways that couldn't be questioned. And the exclamation "We have seen him!" became the foundation upon which Christianity was built. Even today we must continue to "see Christ" through the witness of Scripture and 2,000 years of testimony by those who have been changed by Him. And we continue to "see Him" through our own inner witness and personal experience—saying along with the saints of the ages, "He touched me!" Revelation and our experience of (and witness to) it are still central in the Christian faith.

But Jesus did not stop there. Luke next tells us that He provided *instruction*. During those forty days, Jesus was "speaking of the things pertaining to the kingdom of God" (1:3). Confidence needed to be linked with content. Experience needed to be enriched with information. This is at least one reason why Luke was inspired to record the content of five sermons delivered by early Christian leaders (chapters 7, 10, 13, and 25). Christianity not only warms the heart, it also enlightens the mind. It has substance as well as emotion. And the two work together to create reality.

Luke does not go into detail about the instruction. He simply says that the focal point was "the Kingdom." Linking this with what we know of the Kingdom from biblical teaching, this seems to mean that Jesus wanted to drive home the point that in His coming a new order or fellowship had begun. This was easier to know and experience as long as He was physically present, but the disciples had to know it as truth even in His physical absence. They had to understand that in Christ, God had split history down the middle. From now on everything was to be interpreted in light of Christ's coming. Now, the mission of the disciples was to be that of proclaiming, interpreting, and expanding the Kingdom—that is, helping others come to the place of seeing, experiencing, and living life from that perspective, too.

As the events in the book of Acts unfold, we see this perspective working itself out in the disciples' witnessing and preaching. Today we call it the *kerygma*—the proclamation of the early church. Because we will be reading and studying several sermons in Acts, let's review what the basic elements of the kerygma were so we will recognize them in our study:

Jesus Teaches by Providing Instruction.

15

1. The coming of Jesus fulfills Old Testament prophecy.
2. Jesus is the Messiah and has ushered in God's "new age."
3. The fact of Jesus' resurrection is the main proof of Christianity's truthfulness.
4. Jesus will one day return to establish the Kingdom on earth.
5. The only way to participate in the Kingdom (for time and eternity) is to believe in Jesus as the Saviour.

It's exciting to visualize the disciples meeting daily with Jesus during the forty days between His resurrection and ascension and filling their minds with these truths until their hearts burned to share the Good News with others. Who of us would not have a message to share if the Lord Himself were to teach us in person for forty days as He did the disciples!

One important point to remember is that the Christian message is not something *we* invent. It is something Christ gives. At the end of this forty-day period, the disciples knew *what* they were to share. They didn't have to devise or invent a message; they had only to report it. And the rest of the book of Acts confirms that they did this conscientiously, qualitatively, and enthusiastically. As the early Church began to grow, instruction was an all-important function: "And they continued stedfastly in the apostles' doctrine and fellowship" (2:42) and "...daily in the temple, and in every house, they ceased not to teach and preach Jesus Christ" (5:42).

Unfortunately, this same spirit doesn't prevail today. There is a widespread neglect of serious Bible study, so it is not surprising that many in the church are still "infants" in their knowledge of and ability to share the Christian faith. Far too many people claim to have had some kind of "experience" with Christ, but they are walking proof that experience alone is insufficient. Experience without instruction is shallow enthusiasm and not to be trusted. Instruction without experience is dead intellectualism. Instruction and experience must go together; otherwise there can be no vitality and life.

Jesus Teaches on Sharing the Good News.

But, still, there is more to Jesus' method. There is *impartation:* "Ye shall be witnesses," He said (1:8). Early on, the disciples knew they were to be commissioned to carry on Christ's work. Jesus was appealing to that part of the human personality that responds positively to being involved and needed. Studies in business and industry have shown that worker productivity and efficiency increase when employees feel they are consulted and appreciated. The same is true in the fellowship of faith—the church. As people are actively involved in witnessing and working for the Lord in ministering to the physical and spiritual needs, the church has vitality and comes alive. There is no such thing as a spectator Christian. We are all called to be participants—team players—in living and sharing the Good News of Jesus Christ.

Behind Jesus' method is the idea that every Christian is intended to be a *functioning* member of the Body of Christ. The category of "inactive member" is really a misnomer. It's an institutional attempt to help some people "save face." In actual fact there's only one kind of authentic church member: active and involved. To be a disciple of Christ is to hear the call and respond with action.

Jesus' Teaching and Acting the Good News.

But surely this feeling of anticipation and excitement did not last long before the disciples asked themselves, "How in the world are we ever going to be able to do it?" They knew they couldn't duplicate Jesus' work under their own power. But in response, Jesus promised that His method of impartation also included the indispensable factor, the Holy Spirit: "...ye shall receive power, after that the Holy Ghost is come upon you" (1:8). In promising them the Spirit, Jesus was offering them the same Presence and power that enabled Him to do His work.

We must not get the idea that Jesus accomplished His mission on earth in the flesh. Earlier, Luke had made it plain that Jesus did His work "in the power of the Spirit" (Luke 4:14, 18). And in Jesus' final instructions to His disciples, He made it clear that they would succeed only by the power of the Spirit: "... tarry ye in the city of Jerusalem, until ye be endued with power from on high" (Luke 24:49) and "... wait for the promise of the Father" (Acts 1:4).

It is important that we properly understand what Jesus meant here in relation to our own discipleship. So often the words *tarry* and *wait* have been misinterpreted as a call to passivism. Well-meaning people have sometimes said, "We must not do anything unless we have received the Spirit." But we are living on this side of Pentecost. The Spirit has been given! We don't have to wait for Him to come. He has come and is here.

At the same time, though, we must not be deluded into thinking that all of the pronouncements and actions of Christians and the Church are automatically done "in the Spirit." The pages of history are dotted with tragic stories of people who acted erroneously—at times even perpetrating atrocious cruelties—and claimed to be doing it "in the Spirit." We cannot maintain and expand the ministry of Christ and the Church by operating on a blank check principle that assumes God automatically agrees with decisions simply because a group of Christians made them.

How, then, shall we steer the proper course between these two errors? I believe it comes in recognizing that on the day of Pentecost God dug the well of the Spirit for Christians and the Church in all time. We do not have to wait for a replay of Pentecost. But like the first disciples, we must drink from the well. That is, we must act *after* we have interacted with the Spirit in contemplation and prayer. This is the kind of impartation Jesus gave His disciples: involvement mixed with dependence, happiness linked with humility, participation infused with power.

Jesus' Teaching on Correction.

This part of our lesson also shows that our perspective is gained by another of Jesus' methods: correction. Verses 6 and 7 show that Jesus had to correct a misunderstanding about the Kingdom. Despite the fact that the disciples had been receiving regular and deep instruction about the Kingdom of God, they were still filtering Jesus' words through a Jewish mind-set. For over 400 years the Jews had longed for the coming of the Messiah. But they were convinced that His coming would mean the national and political restoration of the Davidic kingdom to Israel. So their question in verse 6—"...Lord, wilt thou at this time restore again the kingdom to Israel?"—while off-base, is not unusual.

From our perspective we find it hard to understand that after being with Jesus for over three years, after witnessing His death and resurrection, they would still be so blind as to ask such a question. But with infinite patience Jesus tries to help them see that the Kingdom of God takes priority over the kingdom of Israel. They had to understand that building the earthly kingdom is not the same as building the heavenly one. But above all, they had to know that the Kingdom of God is always bigger than our "lesser kingdoms." God's work is always bigger than our understanding of it.

I can remember when I was a teenager hearing people say that any preacher who read his prayer (even if he wrote it himself) was "unspiritual." Real preachers prayed extemporaneously and "from the heart." I uncritically accepted that view until I met some deeply committed Christians who found worship most meaningful through the use of ritual and liturgy. Through them, God expanded my vision of "the Kingdom."

Does this mean that I should abandon my "lesser kingdoms," the personal preferences and priorities that seem important to me? I don't think so. I suspect the apostles continued to pray, as their fathers had, for the deliverance of Jerusalem and the restoration of the Davidic kingdom. But what changed was that they no longer saw the lesser kingdom as the ultimate priority or the only way God could work to accomplish His purposes. We learn from this, I believe, that it is perfectly all right to hold to our perspective and priorities, but we must not be so arrogant as to limit the Kingdom of God to our view of it.

Jesus' Teaching on Assurance.

Our lesson gives us one more element in Jesus' method: assurance. Assurance that they would never labor alone in their task (1:9–11). Even as Jesus' ascension was running its course, angels appeared to assure the disciples that He would "come in like manner as ye have seen him go into heaven" (1:11). And we have the complete picture when we couple this with His last promise: "... lo, I am with you alway, even unto the end of the world" (Matt. 28:20).

Why was this assurance so important to the disciples? Simply because they had to "lose Jesus" again. They had lost Him the first time when He died on the cross. Now they were losing Him as He ascended into heaven and returned to His Father. But there is a difference. They walked down the hill of Calvary alone and lonely. But this time, when they walked down the hill called Olivet, the disciples were alone but not lonely! Even though they would

After spending forty days "speaking of the things pertaining to the kingdom of God" Jesus took His disciples to the top of the Mount of Olives and ascended to heaven from there.

never again walk with Christ in the flesh, they would never again be without the presence of His Spirit.

Those forty days with Jesus between His resurrection and ascension must have been a glorious time of fellowship and learning for the disciples. In a way it was their "senior year" of training before they were sent out on their own. But as with any graduation, it was only the commencement. They would be learners for the rest of their lives. And that learning process was to take on special significance as they left the mount of ascension and returned to their vigil in the upper room in Jerusalem.

For forty days the disciples had been with Jesus in some of the most important, intensive, and intimate times they had ever known. It would have been easy, even understandable, for them to have returned to Jerusalem to merely bask in the warm memories that their time with the Lord had produced. But they didn't. Instead, they attended to several strategic activities that made possible their readiness for the coming of the Spirit.

First of all, they "...continued with one accord in prayer and supplication" (1:14). This implies that the days between the ascension and Pentecost were lived in the atmosphere of prayer. Or to put it another way, the disciples continued (on another level) the communion with Christ that they had experienced during the preceding forty days. This was especially important, for not to have done so would have easily produced the feeling that they were living in a vacuum. Doubts could have begun to creep in. But, through prayer, they stayed connected with the vision and the promise that Jesus had given them.

In C.S. Lewis's masterpiece, *The Screwtape Letters*, he has the senior devil (Screwtape) writing to the junior devil (Wormwood) about how to lead a new convert astray. Screwtape insists that the way to defeat the best efforts of a fledgling convert is to prevent him from feeling the need to pray. And then Screwtape adds that if that doesn't work, Wormwood is to get the convert to concentrate attention on himself rather than on Jesus. Had the disciples turned their gaze from Christ to themselves during those days of waiting, they could have easily fallen prey to discouragement or impatience. By focusing all their attention on Jesus, they were content to wait for the promise they knew was coming.

But we notice that they didn't limit themselves to prayer. They also attended to a very practical matter (1:15–26). Here we see how the disciples dealt with the "gap" in their fellowship that resulted with the demise of Judas. The eleven disciples apparently felt the need to be at full strength in terms of leadership when the Spirit came.

Attending to Business (1:12–26)

A Fellowship of Prayer.

The Fellowship Restored to Full Strength.

From this action we learn two important things about these early Christians—qualities that will serve us well in our own pilgrimage of faith.

First, the 120 or so who were clustered together in the upper room were not "so heavenly minded that they were no earthly good." Even though they were devoted to prayer, they were not "lost in prayer"—they didn't have their heads in the clouds. This is important because true discipleship is not measured by how "other-worldly" we are. Inattentiveness to practical matters is no mark of spirituality. Even the task of choosing next year's leaders is part of faithful discipleship. And on a mundane level, sometimes the most spiritual thing we can do is change a diaper, write a letter, or just take the time to listen—especially take the time to listen!

Brother Lawrence, the seventeenth-century monk who gave us the classic *Practice of the Presence of God*, reinforced this truth by showing us how he finally came to the place in his life where washing dishes in the monastery kitchen was just as much an act of devotion to God as was attending Communion in the monastery chapel. I have come to believe that one of our greatest needs is to tear down the man-made barriers that separate the sacred from the secular. For the Christian, all of life is sacred.

In this act of selecting Judas's successor we also see their concern for excellence of leadership. The only individuals considered were those who had demonstrated their faithfulness from the beginning (1:22). With these qualifications set forth only two candidates emerged. And interestingly, they were two "quiet people." Neither Joseph, called Barsabas, nor Matthias are mentioned before or after this event. Although they were both considered appointable to this great task, by a casting of lots Matthias was selected (1:26).

We learn from this story that the best leaders may not be among those who are most prominent or among those who campaign hardest for the job. True leadership is something we rise to by demonstrating faithfulness and obedience; it isn't something we are given because of charisma or clout.

A United Fellowship.   In reflecting on this part of our lesson it is important to note that the disciples did all these things in close proximity to each other (1:13 and 2:1). I don't think this means they were never separated from one another during these ten days. This was not the world's first Christian commune. It does mean, though, that they recognized their need for each other, and it is likely they were together much of the time. But their unity was not simply one of physical location; it was also of spiritual oneness.

Their being "in one accord" closely parallels Ezekiel's vision of the dry bones (Ezek. 37:1–14). In this vivid picture we see that the next-to-the-last-stage of renewal was the coming together of the bones, complete with sinews and flesh. All that was missing was the breath of the Spirit of God. And when the breath of God came, "they lived, and stood up upon their feet" (Ezek. 37:10).

I get this same picture of the early Christians. Their time with Jesus and with each other had brought them together and had clothed them with the essentials. Only the Spirit was missing. And God graciously provided Him.

The True Beginning. This part of our lesson ends with the true beginning—the beginning of the new fellowship of believers, the Church as God intended it to be (2:1–4). Even though Pentecost was ushered in with the most dramatic of manifestations (wind and tongues of fire), the more profound point must not be lost in the symbolism. Pentecost was God's inbreathing—"they were all filled with the Holy Ghost" (2:4)—which enabled them to minister. Without the infilling of the Holy Spirit nothing else would have really mattered. But with the coming of the Spirit, the Church, like the collection of dry bones in the Ezekiel story, was enabled to march as a mighty and powerful army in the world. And those first-century Christians marched! As we shall see now in our ongoing study, within a few years their gospel of Good News had infiltrated the known world of that time.

As I write this, my family and I are looking forward to a lengthy trip out of the country in a couple of months. But before we can leave we are going through a detailed process of preparation. If we are faithful in our preparation, we'll be ready when the time comes. These opening verses of Acts give us a vivid picture of the disciples' preparation time. Without those days of preparation on their part we might not have been recipients of the gospel in our time.

23

I think the parallel between then and now is clear. We have here our model for action and for the future in this vignette of the "120" in the upper room who, through prayer, fellowship with each other, and empowerment by the Holy Spirit, were prepared to confront the future.

Lord, Thank You for helping me to understand this lesson. AMEN.

WHAT THIS SCRIPTURE MEANS TO ME—Acts 1:1–2:4

It was a hot, sultry August night. We were tired, worn-out, and confused. My wife and I had thought our future was clear, but we faced an unexpected dilemma. In a quiet moment, I found myself wondering if the eleven disciples sitting in an upper room might have felt the same kind of confusion. For, like them, life had taken us to a crossroads.

We had decided to move. Lynn, my wife, had received a generous and well-earned scholarship to a respected university for post-graduate work. But then, with the commitment already made to accept the scholarship and to move 800 miles away to a southern city, I received a challenging new job offer.

Now we faced a new decision, and, like those disciples, we were searching for God's will. Our minds were flooded with questions—what should we do? What part was God playing in all of this?

It's been like that since the beginning of time—people like you and me, walking through their own crossroads, waiting for God to direct them. Dag Hammarskjöld, beset with personal crisis, thought one day that he had reached the limit of his endurance. But soon after that, in 1952, he was elected Secretary-General of the United Nations. And he would later write in his diary that his seemingly great burdens became light only when God placed new demands on him.

It was that way with us. When under God's guidance we decided that we should stay where we were and I should accept the new position, vast new opportunities began opening themselves to us. Lynn was accepted at another school and was invited to become the pastor of a church. Suddenly, we had an exciting new life.

That, though the language may be different, is the message of this Scripture lesson for me. At the same time, it is a map of what we will find throughout the book of Acts and in all of life—in our moments of question and confusion, God's Spirit is there to empower us to overcome and move forward. The next step may seem impossible until suddenly, like a mighty wind, God is there to lead us on.

Can you picture those eleven disciples in the upper room? Since the crucifixion, they had been at times exhilarated, and at other times baffled, by the events which had taken place. Now, their Lord was gone from their presence again, and they stood alone at the crossroads of their lives and ministry.

But then it happened! The Holy Spirit came and filled the room and filled them. What Jesus had promised, happened that night. And that is the startling—and wonderful—revelation of Acts: that the same Comforter the disciples knew is with us as our Guide today.

During my time as an editor and writer for *Guideposts* magazine, I met many Spirit-filled Christians with inspiring stories. But perhaps none have touched me more than two women I met, five years apart. Both are from suburban Chicago, and both had been stricken with potentially fatal diseases. For years they struggled, never knowing whether the next day would be their last. But their faith never faltered—each continued to meet God in any way she could. And in time, each received the healing touch of God. By grace they had waited and God's special gift for them had come, even in the midst of their trials.

Many years before that first Pentecost, an Old Testament prophet wrote, "But they that wait upon the Lord shall renew their strength; they shall mount up with wings as eagles; they shall run, and not be weary; and they shall walk, and not faint" (Isa. 40:31). That is our promise for today—and tomorrow.

LESSON 2
ACTS 2:5–8:3

Growing under Pressure

Heavenly Father, It isn't easy to "grow under pressure," but it's effective! Thank You for giving me opportunities to grow in You. AMEN.

It would be difficult to find a term that more adequately describes the attitude of many than the word *stress*. We are a people under pressure. Almost daily, the medical world adds evidence that shows the negative effects of stress upon the mind and body. The publishing world continues to produce books on how to cope with stress. Even the church is discovering that burnout is real and counterproductive to true spirituality.

Although they didn't use the same terms as we do, the early Christians knew what it was like to live their faith under pressure. In this lesson we will examine some of the pressures they faced and see how they continued to minister and grow in spite of them.

Opportunity Unlimited (2:5–47)

A Unique Opportunity.

Ironically, the first pressure the early Christians faced was the *pressure of opportunity* (2:5–47). We find that God timed the coming of the Holy Spirit with the Jewish celebration of Pentecost. No day, including the Passover, brought more people from all over the world than did the Day of Pentecost (2:5, 9–11). For the Jews it was a time to dedicate the firstfruits of their crops to God. For the Christians it became the "firstfruits" of a new wave of Christian believers who would, in time, grow throughout the world.

In my travels I often fly with businessmen who are criss-crossing the country in search of new and expanded markets. Many of them are laboring under the pressure of opportunity: meeting budgets and quotas, living with increased sales goals, and so on. Although opportunity is a good time to demonstrate one's abilities, it is also a time of high anxiety. The tragedies and implications of failure continually hover over the situation. While the first Christians were not given any daily quotas to meet, they surely recognized the opportunity they had for "reaching the world" in the microcosm of people who were in Jerusalem that day of Pentecost.

Those first Christians wasted no time in *connecting* with the people. The coming of the Spirit supernaturally enabled them to share the gospel in many languages (2:4). Luke tells us that the people who jammed the streets of Jerusalem were from "every nation under heaven," and they were amazed "that every man heard them speak in his own language" (2:5–6). Something very strange was happening as that handful of Galileans witnessed to the "wonderful works of God" with boldness and in a variety of languages.

Although we may not be able to "speak with other tongues" as the first disciples did, we will do well to realize the importance of "speaking the language" others can understand. For us today this will mean taking the time to establish credibility. People are skeptical of "hype" and the fast "come-on." We have much better chances for success in sharing our Christian faith when we do so with caring and compassion, and in a common language that everyone can readily understand.

We also learn from our Scripture lesson that after *connection* had been made with the crowd, *content* was given through the preaching of the first Christian sermon (2:14–36). Here again we see that vital and necessary connection between experience and information. A good illustration of this is seen in the long and effective ministry of Lord Donald Soper, who has witnessed for Christ each week in London's Hyde Park at the famous "speakers' corner." Lord Soper has learned by experience that most of his listeners neither know nor remember the gospel story, and that if

The First Christian Sermon.

they are expected to make an intelligent response to it, they must first of all hear it.

On the Day of Pentecost, the focal point of this part of our lesson, that "hearing" came through Peter's sermon. The twenty-three verses that make up the sermon as Luke has given it to us should be read in your Working Bible more than once as we study and reflect on this lesson. For in this sermon we have a superb model of *kerygma*, one of the four styles of preaching that was prevalent in the early Church. Here is a bold proclamation of the truth of the gospel.

It is also significant, I believe, that this first Christian sermon was delivered by Peter. What a fantastic study in contrasts! Less than two months earlier Peter had turned coward in front of just a few people in the courtyard of the high priest and denied that he was one of Jesus' disciples. But now this same Peter, loved and forgiven by his resurrected Lord and empowered by the Holy Spirit, stood boldly before the masses in Jerusalem and proclaimed that Jesus of Nazareth was indeed the Messiah.

It should also be noted that this sermon is a masterpiece of argument. Because of the joy expressed by the Spirit-filled disciples, their critics accused them of being drunk. But in the beginning of his sermon Peter refutes this by reminding them that it was only 9:00 o'clock in the morning, and then he tells the crowd that what they are seeing is a fulfillment of Joel's prophecy: "And it shall come to pass afterward, that I will pour out my spirit upon all flesh; and your sons and your daughters shall prophesy, your old men shall dream dreams, your young men shall see visions" (Joel 2:28).

We can be sure that Peter's opening words had the attention of the crowd, and from that point on he opened up the Scriptures to prove that Jesus Christ was the fulfillment of the Messianic words of the prophets and that His coming fulfilled their predictions. And then Peter came to his grand climax with the words, "Therefore let all the house of Israel know assuredly, that God hath made that same Jesus, whom ye have crucified, both Lord and Christ" (2:36).

For Luke, here is the clear confirmation of Jesus' words in Acts 1:8. Peter's sermon is a ringing call to the universal proclamation and evangelization that dominates the story in the rest of the book of Acts. Since Luke himself does not personally enter the scene until Acts 16:10, it seems likely that he was a convert to the same kind of message that Peter preached on the Day of Pentecost. His writing is not a dispassionate reporting of historical events; rather, it is the record of one who had himself been transformed by the gospel message.

The Crowd's Response.

Luke now tells us that Peter's message spoke to their hearts and moved them to *conviction*—to a sense of guilt and a recognition of need (2:37–40). Luke's words paint a graphic picture: "Now when they heard this, they were pricked in their heart, and said unto Peter and to the rest of the apostles, Men and brethren, what shall we do?" (2:37). This was an expression of genuine conviction borne out of a dramatic encounter with the Word of God. We see no sign of manipulation here on Peter's part. There is no playing on the emotions of the crowd. Yet, Peter and the rest of the disciples knew that the point of their message announcing the Good News was to call for a response. And as Peter preached, we see him moving closer and closer to the place where those who heard him would have to respond.

Notice that Peter's answer to their question was couched in the atmosphere of repentance: "Repent, and be baptized every one of you in the name of Jesus Christ for the remission of sins..." (2:38). Repentance is fundamental. *Repent* The gospel demands repentance, that is, a turning away from sin. True repentance involves a change of heart and action. When repentance is coupled with baptism (i.e., the rite that speaks of entry into a new way of life), the responders can demonstrate the complete "turning" that is implied in the term *conversion*. And it was this that Peter called for at the end of his sermon.

Several years ago an American theologian had this to say about a witnessing tract that was quite popular at the time: "There's no repentance in it." He pointed out that, by implication, the only thing required was to *receive* Christ, and he correctly reminded us that this is only half of the gospel. In fact, we cannot truly receive Christ until we have first confessed and turned our back on the sin in our lives. This same theologian expressed the opinion that one of the major weaknesses in modern-day Christianity is its attempt to operate on the assumption that you can "have Christ" without making fundamental changes in belief

29

systems, life-styles, and so forth. The first-century Christians made no such assumption.

Next, Luke tells us that those who responded were wholeheartedly welcomed into the *community* (2:41–47). The disciples knew that without immediate and sustained nurturing, their new converts would not hold steady in their faith. Verse 42 tells us exactly what they did to encourage growth and faithfulness: "And they continued stedfastly in the apostles' *doctrine* and *fellowship*, and in *breaking of bread*, and in *prayers*" (italics mine). Verses 44 to 46 tell us that this nurturing also included attention to the physical needs of the whole company of disciples. And in verse 46, especially, we see that their fellowship together as members of God's new society was a joyful one in their worship and in their relationships with each other.

The best-seller, *Megatrends*, by John Naisbitt, has clearly shown that in an age of high technology people still need to feel cared for and given personal attention. Most us have experienced feelings of intense loneliness even when people are close by. We all need the reassurance that we belong—that people care. The current phrase "high tech/ high touch" expresses that need so well.

Luke helps us to see in this part of our lesson that these early Christians demonstrated "high touch" in a very practical way. They "lived out" in their day-to-day relationships a deep concern for each others' physical, emotional, and spiritual needs. In this, they gave us a greatly needed model for today—our needs are essentially the same even though almost 2,000 years separate us from their time. Christianity is not a faith that thrives in isolation. We need each other!

A Response to Need and the Results (3:1–4:22)

When that handful of believers in Jerusalem saw the reactions of the crowd during and immediately following Peter's sermon, they undoubtedly felt the pressure of opportunity. In response to their witness the crowds were asking the right question: "What shall we do?" And in response to an alive and authentic witness for Christ today, that same question is being asked. Behind the masks of smugness and self-sufficiency in our sophisticated society there is a passionate need to be known and cared for and loved. And when those around us see this kind of Christianity in action, they, too, will ask, "What shall we do?"

Christianity doesn't run into much trouble as long as it minds its own business. It is only when Christians begin to influence their surroundings that reaction and opposition set in. To say that what happened at Pentecost "upset the system" is an understatement, but this next part of our lesson (3:1–4:22) underscores the problems that arose, for here we look at the second pressure faced by those early Christians—the *pressure of censure*.

A Cripple Healed.

Luke now moves us quickly into a new drama in which the chief characters are Peter and John and an unnamed man who was so severely crippled that he could not walk at all. The setting was the temple, and the time was the ninth hour of the Jewish day—three in the afternoon. It was the time of evening prayer or sacrifice. Peter and John were obviously following their regularly established custom of going to the temple for worship at this hour.

While there, they were confronted at the temple gate by a crippled beggar who asked them for alms (3:2–3). The scene next moves with breathtaking speed to its climax, for Luke tells us that Peter turned full attention on the needy man and said, "Silver and gold have I none; but such as I have give I thee: In the name of Jesus Christ of Nazareth rise up and walk" (3:4–6).

Having said that Peter reached out and touched him—"....lifted him up...And he leaping up stood, and walked, and entered with them into the temple, walking, and leaping, and praising God" (3:7–8). Peter and John were used at that moment by the Spirit of God to give the crowd an object lesson on the power that was unleashed on the world by Jesus Christ through His death and resurrection.

Power

Peter and John saw a man with a deep need while they were "on their way" to worship and pray. They didn't view this crippled beggar as an interruption but as an opportunity, and they acted to meet his need. But in doing so, they created quite a commotion, for the crowd was "filled with wonder and amazement...greatly wondering" (3:10–11).

Before going on, I want to stress an important point. So often we structure our lives with rather fixed agendas. We set goals for what we think we want to do and should do. Then if, unexpectedly, someone or something diverts our attention, we tend to become impatient or possibly even angry—we've been distracted and interrupted. But again and again Jesus gave us our model for action—no person in need is ever an interruption!

Peter's Second Sermon.

It was the upheaval in the crowd over the healing of the crippled man that prompted Peter's second sermon in Luke's sequence of events (3:12–26).

With a boldness that matched the climate of his first sermon on the Day of Pentecost, Peter indicted his listeners for their rejection of Jesus and for their role in His crucifixion. But at the same time Peter signaled Jesus' victory over evil through His resurrection. And again he gives a ringing call for repentance. Peter then closes his moving appeal by reminding them of God's covenant with Abraham and adds, "Unto you first God, having raised up his Son Jesus, sent him to bless you, in turning away every one of you from his iniquities" (3:26).

Peter and John Arrested.

This sermon of Peter's invoked two kinds of responses (4:1–4). The priests, the captain of the temple, and the Sadducees descended angrily on the scene, arrested Peter and John because of their word that Jesus had been raised from the dead, and threw them into jail overnight until they could appear before the Sanhedrin.

Now, as then, obedience to the teaching of Jesus and adherence to the Christian faith produces opposition of one kind or another. For some, that opposition may be social, mental, or emotional. For others, even today, it may involve physical restriction or even prison. To not follow the secular status quo isn't popular. But just as the previous part of our lesson gave us an understanding of how to handle positive opportunity, we are now given insight as to how to deal with negative resistance.

On Trial.

The scene shifts next to the following morning and to the meeting hall of the Jewish Sanhedrin. After being placed on the witness stand, the disciples were asked, "By what power, or by what name, have ye done this?" (4:7). In response, Peter launched into an explanation (4:8–12).

First, we see that Peter was courteous. He addressed the Sanhedrin in formal, polite terms. We might describe him as "cool and collected." But that is the way it is when the

Holy Spirit is in control, and Luke tells us that Peter was "filled with the Holy Ghost" (4:8). Again, we see a sharp contrast to Peter's uncontrolled behavior in the Garden of Gethsemane when he lashed out with a sword against the opposition (John 18:10). This simple difference in action is a profound demonstration of the change that had occurred in Peter's life.

This change in Peter is an illustration of Jesus' words, "Blessed are the meek: for they shall inherit the earth" (Matt. 5:5). The term for "meek" in the Greek of the New Testament means "one who demonstrates power under control." Peter's calmer response is no indication of passivity, unconcern, or even fatigue after an uncomfortable night in jail. Rather, it is the attitude of one confidently bearing witness to his Lord in the power of the Holy Spirit.

I confess this has been a struggle for me. In my zeal to witness for Christ, I have at times let my emotions override my intellect. Agitation and even anger have clouded my ability to deal rationally and lovingly with those who do not agree with me. Unfortunately, this happens too often, even in our Christian world. But in this scene Peter is a model of courtesy.

By being "under control," by maintaining a calm and courteous spirit, Peter was better able to give a good defense of his faith. And Peter opened his defense by showing the benefits of the faith and its excellence over other ways of life: a "good deed done to the impotent man" (4:9).

This witness to excellence must characterize our interaction with the world around us. It involves excellence of both character and action. This is important because critics of our Christian faith will be quick to see through inconsistencies between our expressions of faith and our actions. As Christians, we must keep close watch on our lives and witness to make certain that we are an encouragement to others in their search for faith.

In closing his arguments to the Sanhedrin, Peter made the way of salvation clear for them and us when he said, "Neither is there salvation in any other: for there is none other name under heaven given among men, whereby we must be saved" (4:12). And while we see from the rest of the scene that Peter's witness didn't change their minds, Luke tells us that they marveled at the boldness of Peter and John and "took knowledge of them, that they had been with Jesus" (4:13). What a great tribute to the credibility of the two disciples!

But while the Jewish religious leaders were not won over by either Peter's witness or the sight of the healed former cripple, we read that "they could say nothing against it" (4:14). They couldn't deny the miracle or the strength of Peter's words, but they could try to keep it quiet—to keep Peter and John from speaking and teaching "in the name of Jesus." But Peter's response was clear: their actions would not be regulated by legal decree (4:19–20).

There will undoubtedly be those times when we, as Christians, feel the pressure of opposition. But I believe the qualities demonstrated by Peter and John in this scene can be of help to us as we attempt to handle opposition wherever it may be found. As with the first disciples, the real issue is not *whether* to witness, for, like Peter and John, "...we cannot but speak the things which we have seen and heard" (4:20). Instead, the real issue is *how* to witness. But we can be certain that when we are sensitive to the Holy Spirit, He will provide not only the opportunity for witness, but also the proper attitude and approach.

The Jerusalem Church under Fire (4:23–6:7)

Peter and John's Report.

As soon as Peter and John were released from custody, they "went to their own company, and reported all that the chief priests and elders had said unto them" (4:23). And following that we have their prayer (4:24–30), their grand affirmation of trust in the Lord and their determination to speak boldly and to act in the name of Jesus.

A Powerful Unity.

Even though the believers then received unusual assurance of the power and providence of God in their behalf (4:31), they did not assume a passive posture when it came to taking care of each other's needs—spiritual confidence was linked with material concern. They were drawn together in a powerful unity that Luke says caused them to have "all things common" (4:32). Because of this open spirit among them, no one lacked for anything.

This action by the early Christians has been one of the most controversial parts of the book of Acts. The most common question asked is: "Does the Bible teach a sort of Christian communism?" The answer to this must be a quick, clear, "No!" Even a casual student of communism will know that it operates out of an atheistic presupposition. Actually, the mutual sharing of goods was a direct result of the activity of God in the hearts of the people. Theirs was not a humanitarianism based simply on noble philosophy or high human motives; it was inspired and directed by the Spirit of God.

A related question is: "Does the Bible in this scene teach a Christian commune-ism?" Does it imply that all Christians should sell their possessions and band together in some kind of communal living? Here again, the answer is "No." As far as we can tell from the New Testament story of the development of the early Church, the Jerusalem church was the only one that took this approach. Other congregations met their responsibility to the needy in other ways.

This raises a final question: "Are we then exempted from this particular teaching?" And once again, the answer is, "No." We are not exempted. But to apply the lesson properly we must distinguish between the *specific* ministry described here and the universal truth it conveys. While no other church in the New Testament seems to have adopted the Jerusalem model, they all demonstrated the same concern for one another. This truth is underlined by Paul in 1 Corinthians 12:25–26: "That there should be no schism in the body; but that the members should have the same care one for another. And whether one member suffer, all the members suffer with it; or one member be honored, all the members rejoice with it."

We find in this a principle that is important to us today. In too many churches we not only fail to provide for the needs of others in the congregation, we don't even know their names. The early Church was a community of believers who knew and cared for each other. And even though the church in Jerusalem now had several thousand members, a way was found to know those who were in need and minister to them.

At the same time, the book of Acts is very realistic. In 6:1–8, we see that this system, though admirable, was not perfect. Even though this takes us out of the natural sequence, take a moment now and read those verses in your Working Bible. Luke shows us here how the Christian community responded when its program was inadequate. The Greek-speaking Jewish converts complained that they were being overlooked in the daily distribution. They appealed for attention and support, and the church responded. In doing so, we see two important principles for us today.

First, the believers stopped any form of preferential treatment. Cultural, linguistic, and racial differences were not allowed to determine the distribution of aid. And second, they took action to put priorities in perspective. If everyone was involved in the daily distribution, the tasks of prayer and the ministry of the Word would collapse. Some division of labor was needed so the apostles could be free to devote themselves to prayer and the Word. To meet the needs of the community, a new order of men with good reputations, who were wise and full of the Holy Ghost, was formed. They were called deacons, and Stephen was part of this group.

I once heard the president of a large corporation say that if most businesses in the United States were run like churches, our economic system would collapse in a year. In a way, he was reinforcing the need for a "division of labor" in the Body of Christ that we find here in the Jerusalem church.

I'm not suggesting that we adopt secular management techniques in a wholesale and uncritical fashion. Rather, I believe that we might well learn something helpful about "division of labor" on a church level. For example, if trained lay persons handled the administrative tasks, ordained ministers could concentrate their talents on ministry of the Word, prayer, and counseling. For everyone, it would mean a new commitment to a broad-based ministry. And in the long run, it could meet the needs of the people in the Body of Christ more efficiently.

Deception at Work.
The book of Acts never glosses over the imperfection of Christians. This adds to the sense of realism we get when we read it. As soon as the early Christians had dealt with the pressure of providing for those in need, they then had to turn their attention to handling the pressure of deception (5:1–11).

Here is a vivid story of deceit and dishonesty. The problem of Ananias and Sapphira was not that they withheld part of their money for themselves. There is no indication that believers were forced to put everything in a pool for the common support. Rather, the problem was that they lied to the church by implying that what they gave was all they had. It was the lie, not the amount, that brought the condemnation. Peter's words were very strong: "Ananias, why hath Satan filled thine heart to lie to the Holy Ghost.... thou hast not lied unto men, but unto God" (5:3–4).

I suspect that the story of Ananias and Sapphira is repeated frequently in the Christian community. Maybe not in the specifics, but in the spirit. The condemnation was that Ananias and Sapphira wanted to look like "total givers" when in fact they were not. This Scripture lesson is a double warning to us today. First, it warns us not to become enamored of or dependent upon the so-called big givers. They may not be giving as much as we think, or they may not be giving in the right spirit. And second, we need to prayerfully check our motive for giving.

The proper spirit for giving is described by Jesus in the story of the widow's mite (Luke 21:1–4). While she gave all she had, it wasn't much. It was the spirit in which she gave that mattered to Jesus, not the amount. Luke may well have had that story in mind as he wrote about the deception of Ananias and Sapphira. These two stories illustrate the sacredness of our stewardship. Our giving to the Lord and His cause is not done to impress people or for income tax deduction—it is a sacred matter between ourselves and God. To be dishonest, to give with a wrong spirit, is to fall prey to the pressure of deception.

Faith Under Fire.

As we read and study this part of our lesson, we begin to sense the progression of intensity that Luke is describing. Beginning with the positive pressure of opportunity, we have now moved to the actual pressure of confinement. Even as the church was growing rapidly (5:12–16) and many miracles were being performed, the Jewish leaders stepped in with their most forceful resistance to date. They "laid their hands on the apostles, and put them in the common prison" (5:18).

Why were they jailed? Surely it was not because people were healed or the kingdom of God was advanced. The issue here is much more subtle. The "indignation" (5:17) of the leaders occurred because the apostles continued to teach in Jesus' name and were "bypassing the system." Their movement was "unofficial" and should be squelched even if some good was coming out of it.

37

This section in Acts 5:12–42 reveals some very important lessons for us. First, we need to face the truth that God isn't limited in the ways He acts. He may do it "our way" or He may do it in a completely new and different way. God is not limited by our understanding of Him. But the Jewish leaders based all their assumptions on the idea that God was bound to act through the approved religious system or at least in ways predictably consistent with the Jewish tradition. The assumption was wrong. By holding tenaciously to that assumption, the religious leaders not only remained blind but also actually worked against the purposes of God!

The second lesson for us here is expressed in the words of the apostles themselves: "We ought to obey God rather than men" (5:29). This was not a super-pious statement made to impress anybody. Instead, it was an honest statement of their conviction and was the result of a long period of walking with Jesus Himself and being instructed by Him after the resurrection. By the time they said these words, they knew to whom they belonged and to what they were called. They were firm in their belief, but it was a firmness based on fact, not stubbornness.

I recently heard the story of a woman who obstinately refused to stop teaching a Sunday school class, claiming she had "the gift of teaching." When her role was questioned by church leaders, she adapted the words of Peter to the situation. It sounded good, but it masked the truth. Unfortunately, she didn't have the gift of teaching and her Christian peers were trying to tell her so.

Stubbornness isn't a mark of spirituality, but deep commitment is. And that is what the disciples exhibited on this occasion. I think it is important to notice, too, that they were talking in this instance to unbelievers and not to their own brothers and sisters in Christ.

At any rate, we see that God honored their courage and they were delivered from prison (5:19). This kind of confirmation left no doubt about what position they should take before their accusers. We can believe that when our response is correct and in the right spirit, it will be confirmed in some way by God. If we are truly "obeying God rather than men," we shall obey Him when He tells us to stick to our guns, and we shall obey Him when He shows us we are wrong and need to confess it.

Again, Peter and the other apostles gave their accusers a forthright witness of the Saviourhood of Jesus and to the power of the Holy Spirit. But Luke tells us they were "cut to the heart" (5:33) and discussed their intention of killing the apostles. Now the story takes an interesting turn. Gamaliel, a widely loved member of the Sanhedrin, and a Pharisee, attempted wisely to intervene and prevent violence. Likening this to certain other recent events, he offers good advice: "...if this counsel or this work be of men, it will come to nought: But if it be of God, ye cannot overthrow it" (5:38–39). In this instance, the group agreed with Gamaliel and released the apostles with only a beating and an admonition to keep quiet.

Running through the narrative is an interesting possibility. Gamaliel was the very person who had given instruction to Saul of Tarsus. And we know from the last part of this lesson that Saul was present at the stoning of Stephen. It is even possible he witnessed this scene we've been discussing. The point is simply this: Long before the apostles ever knew that their faith was having any impact on the opposition, it was!

The final pressure faced by the early Christians was that of martyrdom as demonstrated by Stephen in Acts 6:8–8:3. The fact that Luke devotes so much space to this event reveals its importance then and now. Basilea Schlink, founder of the Evangelical Sisterhood of Mary with headquarters in Germany, has said that more people will be martyred for their faith in the twentieth century than in all the previous centuries combined. So as we read these words in Acts, we hear a message that is significant for us even today.

Faithful unto Death (6:1–8:3)

The first thing of importance to us here is to see the sinister and active nature of evil (6:8–12). When Stephen's opponents in debate in the synagogue saw that they were beaten, they dredged up some witnesses who perjured themselves by claiming that Stephen made certain heretical statements. Based on this flimsy evidence, Stephen was arrested and taken before the Sanhedrin. But as we shall see, the power of evil, though immediately victorious, could not thwart the spread of the gospel.

The second thing of importance to us is to notice that

The First Christian Martyr.

Stephen was prepared. He was ready in attitude and countenance (6:15), and he was ready in message and content (7:1–53). The sermon he preached followed a similar course with those we've already seen in this lesson. And it had a similar outcome, only this time the consequences were more severe. The contrast between Stephen and his listeners is glaring (7:54–60). His listeners were full of hatred; Stephen was full of the Holy Spirit. His listeners were intent on murder; Stephen was intent on forgiving. They called on their anger; he called on his God. They departed in rage, he died in peace—the first Christian martyr.

And Saul of Tarsus saw it all! In fact, there are those who believe that Saul played some kind of role in the dastardly event (7:58). That Luke saw fit to add in 8:1 that "Saul was consenting unto his [Stephen's] death" makes this all the more probable. As we view this whole event from our perspective today, it is clear that Saul's presence and possible participation in the affair was used by God to impact his life and prepare him for his forthcoming conversion. St. Augustine was correct when he wrote, "The church owes Paul to the prayer of Stephen."

The events in this lesson remind me that it is too easy to think that growth takes place in times of security and ease. More than that, it is easy to interpret comfort and prosperity as signs of God's blessing. Clearly God's blessing was on the Church during this time, but it was still a difficult time. Yet, the final message is one of hope: _You can grow under pressure_. In fact, it seems that most of the time our growth and maturity come when we are under pressure.

The "pressures" I experience in my life pale in comparison to the early Christians. Help me to find hope in suffering. AMEN.

WHAT THIS SCRIPTURE MEANS TO ME—Acts 2:5–8:3

The huge, brick United Methodist church had stood on the same street corner in the Bedford-Stuyvesant section of Brooklyn for nearly 125 years. It had been the center of the neighborhood even as wave after wave of new immigrants took up residence in the aging brownstones that surrounded it. And always, the doors stood open as a welcome haven in a city of great need.

Until last November. Late one Saturday night, fire ravaged the old structure. By daybreak, only one charred wall stood guard over the smoldering ruins.

If this were a story of a factory or business, there might be no more to tell. But because we know the beginning of this particular story—the story of God's church that we read about in this lesson—we also know that even the great loss of a burned-down church building cannot bury the spirit and passion of God's people. And in Brooklyn, that is just what happened! That Sunday morning, their tears barely dry, the members of that church sang of God's love and grace, and said afterwards that there was no question but that their church would live on.

"The church," the great theologian Martin Luther once said, "is an *ecclesia*, a congregation, a community of people as in the first century. It is a continuing community of people in whom the Lord is still alive and with whom the Lord is present."

As in the first century, Luther says. That's the model we can hold up for today. It was God's Spirit that energized those early Christians, that gave them the will to go on in spite of heavy persecution and threadbare resources. They had an undeniable promise that kept them going—and we still have that promise today—that the power of God to heal and transform lives is too great to leave unsaid. No matter what.

It was true that first Pentecost day. It was true last November in Brooklyn. And it was true three years ago in a small country village when a bomb blast blew out the rear wall and collapsed the roof of Christ the King Catholic Church.

The day after this tragic event, the pastor of the First Presbyterian Church across Scroggy Road went over to help clean up the mess. And later, on Christmas, Father Kevin Mullan came to wish his Presbyterian neighbors the peace of the season—the Rev. David Armstrong did the same for the Catholic congregation.

What makes this at all remarkable is that Scroggy Road runs through the town of Limavady in Northern Ireland. As a Catholic and Protestant, Father Mullan and the Rev. Armstrong were supposed to be at odds with one another. But when asked about that, their answers were notably similar. They felt compelled, they said, to live the message of Christ. And if that meant they would be standing against the bigotry of those around them, if it meant they were literally putting their lives on the line, then God would help them endure. "I have set the Lord always before me: because he is at my right hand, I shall not be moved" (Psa. 16:8). Peter echoed the Psalmist's words at the first Pentecost. And Father Mullan and Rev. Armstrong live them out today in Northern Ireland.

Living lives that witness to God's power was the challenge and privilege of the early Church in Acts. And throughout the ages, people of God have lived lives of joyful and determined witness to God's love, power, and peace. They, like Peter and the Psalmist, would "not be moved."

Today, the privilege is ours. His love is still the cornerstone on which we can base our lives.

"I sought the greatness and genius of America in her commodious harbors and ample rivers," wrote French historian Alexis deTocqueville 150 years ago, "and it was not there. I sought for the greatness and genius of America in her fertile fields and boundless forests,...in her institutions of learning, and it was not there. Not until I went into the churches of America and heard her pulpits flame with righteousness did I understand the secret of her genius and her power."

The challenges of those early Christians are now ours. We are the carriers of the Apostles' flame for our time.

LESSON 3
ACTS 8:4—12:25

Expanding the Territory

God, Help me to expand my own territory—to tell more and more people about Your love. AMEN.

God never intended for the Christian movement to be confined to Jerusalem. I believe the disciples knew that. On at least two occasions, Jesus had challenged them with a "world vision" (Matt. 28:19 and Acts 1:8). It is also possible that during that forty-day teaching and preparation period between the resurrection and His ascension, Jesus shared with His disciples the vision of the expansion of the Christian faith. Whether or not He gave them a specific plan for that expansion can be only a matter of speculation since the Scripture lesson doesn't give us a clue.

What we do know as we study this lesson is that we have come to the beginning of the second major movement of the book of Acts. Using Acts 1:8 as a key verse for understanding the book, we know that Jesus predicted the spread of Christianity from Jerusalem, to Judea and Samaria, and ultimately to the ends of the earth: "...ye shall be witnesses unto me both in Jerusalem, and in all Judea, and in Samaria, and unto the uttermost part of the earth."

The events in the first seven chapters of Acts confine Christian activity largely to Jerusalem. In our lesson now, though, we see the Good News spreading throughout Judea and into Samaria. Here we see the Church on the move.

Never again would geographical, racial, or cultural boundaries impede the movement of God's new fellowship.

As we study this lesson, I believe it is possible to find an organizing verse in Acts 8:4: "...they that were scattered abroad went every where preaching the word." Luke is showing us here, through the ministry of several key people, how the Church expanded its territory under the leadership of the Spirit. And from this, I believe, we shall discover certain strategies that can help us as we seek to expand the Christian faith in our day.

But first, we need to look at the circumstances that precipitated this moving-out process. Luke tells us that the stoning of Stephen was the beginning of "a great persecution against the church" (8:1), and then he adds, "As for Saul, he made havock of the church, entering into every house, and haling men and women committed them to prison" (8:3). Here is a picture of brutality. The harassment of the Christians was ferocious—they were dragged from their homes and thrown into prison (8:3).

great Persecution of Christians

It was this violent persecution that forced the Christians to leave Jerusalem and seek refuge in the surrounding countryside of Judea and Samaria. But remember, the Jerusalem church membership already ran into the thousands. This was no small exodus—it was a mass migration, an event of significance. And its significance is increased when we read that even though they were a persecuted people, they did not shrink from preaching and teaching about Jesus wherever they went.

What an amazing sequence of events! In an effort to squelch the Christian witness Stephen is killed and Saul of Tarsus tries to throw all the Christians into prison or frighten them into silence. But instead the apostles continued their witness boldly in Jerusalem while thousands of other Christians moved out to infiltrate the surrounding countryside.

Luke's selection of characters in this drama is important to the story. Three men—Philip, Peter, and Paul—stand out above everyone else. Not only were they three outstanding leaders, they were also three examples of the Spirit's ability to use people. Peter, of course, was representative of the apostles—the established ministry of the time. These were the "ordained clergy." Philip was one of the "new ministers," one of the seven deacons referred to in chapter six. And there was Paul, probably selected as a prime example of how God can use the most unlikely people in His service. To me, these lead characters in the Christian drama symbolize the traditional, the innovative, and the surprising ways God works to accomplish His will.

There's an old phrase that asks, "Yes, but will it play in Peoria?" It is meant to describe something that works in one place, but might not in another. That's the question Acts 8:5–40 answers.

No sooner had the Christian believers been dispersed than Philip went "to the city of Samaria, and preached Christ unto them" (8:5). It is quite likely this refers to Samaria's principal city of that time—the ancient city of Samaria that had been rebuilt by Herod and renamed Sebaste. But the important thing to note here is that Philip boldly went with his message of salvation into an area where the people were violently antagonistic to anything related to Judaism, and that would have included Christianity at that time. The bitter hostility between Jews and Samaritans was several hundred years old.

It is for this reason that Philip's move into Samaria had particular significance. It was a landmark event because it proved that the gospel was not just for a select number of Jerusalem Jews but was for everyone—even Samaritans.

It is equally remarkable to see the widespread reception to Philip's message and actions on the part of the Samaritans (8:6–8). But this is just another indication of the radical newness of Christianity. New Christians (converted Jews) were going places they had previously avoided and were sharing their Good News with people they had previously despised. And they were received with open arms! In fact, Luke says, "And there was great joy in that city" (8:8). The Samaritans passed a true test of Christianity—they were full of joy. Then and now authentic Christianity produces people who are full of joy, not of doom and gloom.

In the midst of this joyful setting a minor character entered the scene. His name was Simon, and he was a magician, a sorcerer. Luke indicates that as a result of Philip's preaching Simon became a believer and was baptized

The Glorious Gospel (8:4–8:40)

The Gospel in Samaria.

gospel for all

45

(8:13). Philip apparently felt that his conversion was genuine, and since Simon already had a following because of his reputation (8:9), he could have a positive influence. At this point in the story Luke tells us that Simon "continued with Philip, and wondered, beholding the miracles and signs which were done" (8:13).

But it wasn't long before things changed. When the apostles back in Jerusalem got word about what was happening in Samaria, they sent Peter and John to confirm and affirm the results of Philip's ministry (8:14). After seeing what had happened, Peter and John prayed that the new Samaritan converts would receive the Holy Spirit, and, as Luke writes, the apostles "laid their hands on them, and they received the Holy Ghost" (8:17).

The laying on of hands by Peter and John and the reception of the Holy Spirit by the new converts made a strong impression on Simon. This exceeded anything he'd ever been able to do as a magician, and his baser instincts rose to the surface. Offering Peter and John money, he asked, "Give me also this power, that on whomsoever I lay hands, he may receive the Holy Ghost" (8:19).

Peter's response to Simon (8:20–23) as it comes to us through the King James text is a strong denunciation. The gift of the Holy Spirit was not for sale.

We might title this part of our Scripture lesson, "Glorious, but Not for Sale." Simon's real tragedy was not that he had asked (though that's bad enough); instead, it was that he had thought the power of God could be purchased with human means. He had failed to see that what was happening was not the property of any person—it was the activity of a sovereign God. Two thousand years later we still need to remember that. There's not enough money in the world to get a corner on God's blessing and on the work of the Holy Spirit. The Spirit still moves where and when He wills.

We leave this tragic scene with Simon crying for mercy (8:24–25). While Simon's words here may indicate repentance, we do not know for sure. But we do know that from his name comes our modern term *simony*—the making of profit from sacred things—a despicable act now even as it was then.

Our Scripture lesson further tells us that the gospel continued to produce converts in other Samaritan cities (8:25).

And so, the answer to the question asked at the beginning of this section is, "Yes, it *will* play in Peoria!" The gospel of Jesus Christ is effective wherever it goes in spite of problems and even perversions. The picture of the Christian Church for almost 2,000 years has often been blurred and discolored by the words and actions of people who dishonor the spirit of Jesus. And at times certain groups within the Church have resorted to physical and verbal violence in so-called defense of the faith. But in the face of human sin, God is still in charge; His purposes and will prevails.

Luke now moves us abruptly from Samaria south to a busy highway. We read: "And the angel of the Lord spake unto Philip, saying, Arise, and go toward the south unto the way that goeth down from Jerusalem unto Gaza, which is desert" (8:26). The road Luke is referring to moved south and west from Jerusalem by way of Bethlehem and Hebron and continued on southwest toward the coast where it connected below Gaza with the highly traveled highway to Egypt.

The Gospel to Gaza and Ethiopia.

It was to this highway that Philip was instructed to go. Philip apparently had no idea why he was going; he was merely told to go. And he did. What a marvelous lesson in obedience! Most of us, I'm sure, would have argued with the angel. We would have wanted a plan of action. But God doesn't always work that way; in Philip we have a model for obeying the word of the Lord without question.

The scene shifts now to the desert highway. And it was there Philip came upon an Ethiopian who was sitting in his chariot and reading from an Isaiah scroll. With his careful attention to details Luke tells us that the Ethiopian was a eunuch and attached to the court of Candace as the royal treasurer. The Ethiopia mentioned here is not located where we know it today, but was situated on the Nile River in what is now Sudan.

Philip was next instructed by the Spirit of the Lord to join the man in the chariot. He did, and then follows the story in which Philip explained the Scripture to his fellow traveler. This led to the Ethiopian's conversion and baptism (8:28–39). And from there, through this new convert, the gospel spread toward the heart of Africa.

There are many obvious lessons to be drawn from this

story. But I want to focus especially at the point of our responsiveness to the Holy Spirit. We see that Philip was led by the Spirit in this rendezvous with the Ethiopian. And most certainly, one key to our discipleship is our willingness to listen to and to heed the "nudges" of the Spirit. As we obey those nudges—that guidance—we, too, may be led to be of help, a witness, to people in need. Along with Philip we will have the opportunity to point a searcher toward Jesus Christ.

A friend of mine was recently hospitalized for surgery. During his days of recovery he realized that the person in the next bed was struggling with his faith. In the hours and days that followed, my friend, in response to the guidance of the Spirit, was able to share his experience with his roommate and lead him back to a personal faith in Christ.

If my friend had been concerned only with his own comfort and feelings, he would have missed a divine opportunity. However, because he was open to the Spirit and sensitive to others, he was used by God in a profound way. The challenge for us here is to break out of our self-preoccupation and to live in the presence of the Spirit who is able to use us in new and exciting ways.

Through Philip, Luke has shown us a glorious gospel of Good News—one that works when it is applied. This is not to say that we will always ride the crest of success. There will be down moments of resistance and difficulty. But this part of our lesson provides ample hope for us to believe that Christianity can reach people where they are and bring them into a saving relationship with God.

A Sudden and Surprising Surrender (9:1–9:31)

Twice before, Luke, in line with his unique literary style, has planted mention of a man who now becomes the central figure in one of the greatest dramas in Christian history (9:1–8). We first met Saul when he witnessed Stephen's death. He is then described as creating havoc within the Christian community. Now Luke moves him onto center stage "...breathing out threatenings and slaughter against the disciples of the Lord" (9:1).

A Mission of Vengeance.

But Saul of Tarsus was no ordinary religious fanatic. Born in Tarsus in Cilicia, young Saul had been raised in an intellectual atmosphere flavored with Greek thought and rich in the culture of this ancient city. From such a rich background he would have been able to draw from the noblest teaching in the Graeco-Roman world.

From that heritage Saul moved on to Jerusalem where he became a student of Rabbi Gamaliel, one of the greatest Jewish teachers of that time. It isn't surprising that Saul advanced rapidly, and as a zealous Pharisee, he had become a sworn enemy of the Christians.

It is apparent that some Jewish Christians had migrated to the city of Damascus, at that time an independent metropolis situated within the boundaries of the Nabatean kingdom. Obviously, Saul had heard about this Christian community and, armed with papers of extradition, he set out to apprehend them and bring them back to Jerusalem for punishment.

It is quite likely that Saul's route on this mission of vengeance took him north from Jerusalem through Samaria to just south of the Sea of Galilee where he crossed the Jordan River. It is likely that he headed north through the vicinity of Gadara and over the Golan Heights, where he would then have moved north and east toward Damascus. In all, the distance was probably between 135 and 150 miles and would have involved six to eight days of rather rigorous travel. The strenuousness of the journey indicates Saul's vehemence.

A Dramatic Confrontation.

Saul of Tarsus is without doubt the last person mentioned so far that we would expect to become a Christian. Yet Luke tells us that as Saul and his party were getting close to Damascus, he had a dramatic confrontation with One who identified Himself as "Jesus whom thou persecutest" (9:5). And out of that bright light Jesus added, "It is hard for thee to kick against the pricks." Saul's excessive and compulsive zeal and anger may well have been the outward sign of inner torture. There's much about the Saul of those days that we don't know, but we do know that on that Damascus road the grace of God shone brightly and Saul was converted.

This, of course, is a familiar story to Christians everywhere. Unfortunately, some have used it across the years as the "model" for all conversions. There is much cause for us to rejoice in Saul's experience, however, it is wrong to consider it normal for everyone else. What is normal, though, is the ability of God to break through even the most hostile and stubborn defenses and to win us to Himself. This event is a marvelous reminder that no one is beyond the reach of God!

In this next part of our story (9:10–19) we come to the confirmation of what happened. It was absolutely necessary that outside confirmation be given to Saul's conversion. Let's look at how this was worked out.

In response to Saul's question, "What wilt thou have me to do?" (9:6), the Lord told him to go into Damascus and wait for further instructions. This he did, but since he had been blinded by his encounter with God, he had to be led in by those who were with him. And Luke next tells us that he waited three days—blind, refusing to eat or drink—before he received any further word.

The Lord's Special Messenger.

Once again the scene shifts, and it goes to a man named Ananias, a resident of Damascus, who the Lord had selected to be the one to confirm the conversion of Saul (9:10–18). It is hard for us to realize how much Ananias risked in obeying the Lord and going to Saul. He put his life on the line in approaching the very person who was arresting and imprisoning Christians.

I'm quite sure he was willing to obey the Lord and go to Straight Street because he was a man of prayer. Ananias had to know a deep level of communion with God to be willing to take the risk involved. I find it very interesting to compare the dialogue here between God and Ananias (9:11–16) with the conversation between God and Moses in Exodus 3. Take just a minute and turn back to the third chapter of Exodus and make the comparison. The outcome is much the same, isn't it? In both of these stories we receive our own confirmation of the truth that when God gives us an assignment, we can be sure that He will give us whatever it takes to complete that assignment.

Imagine, if you can, this next scene. Saul has been waiting—alone. His world has been turned upside down. What would happen next? The door opens, and he hears someone walking up to him. Silence. And then, *"Brother Saul*, the Lord, even Jesus, that appeared unto thee in the way as thou camest, hath sent me, that thou mightest receive thy sight, and be filled with the Holy Ghost"

(9:17, italics mine). Once Saul had been an enemy; now he is a brother.

The Rest of the Story.

Luke seems to hurry on as if he can't wait to tell us the rest of the story. Saul receives his sight back, he is physically restored, and enjoys a newfound fellowship with the other believers in Damascus—his new status as a brother in Christ is affirmed by them.

Then we come to the final confirmation of what happened through Saul's own testimony: "And straightway he preached Christ in the synagogues, that he is the Son of God" (9:20). That certainly signals the completeness of Saul's conversion—he preached Christ to the very people who had once been his allies in hating Christians. Their response was understandable (9:21). But Saul held steady with his message, "...and confounded the Jews which dwelt in Damascus, proving that this is very Christ" (9:22).

We move now to the next part of the story—the challenge. It was only a matter of time until Saul's old cronies had taken all they could. An ominous note is sounded as Luke writes, "...the Jews took counsel to kill him" (9:23). Silencing the opposition has always been a tactic of evil. Just recently I read that it is estimated there are at least 20,000 people imprisoned somewhere in the world simply because they are Christians. Still others have been ostracized by their families and friends because they have become Christians. The challenge then and now is inevitable—in Saul's case it was extreme.

But God was just beginning his work with Saul, and so the plans of his enemies were frustrated and he escaped (9:24–25). His problems weren't over just yet, however; he still had to face the challenge of acceptance by the Christians in Jerusalem (9:26–31).

Here were people who had felt the sting of Saul's persecution. It is likely that many had seen him standing in approval at the death of Stephen. They could remember firsthand his threats and violent acts. It is not surprising they were afraid and unwilling to accept him.

Once again it was necessary for someone to vouch for Saul's legitimacy. This time it was Barnabas who pleaded Saul's case (9:27). And this was the beginning of a long relationship between Saul and Barnabas that God would use to spread the gospel. Obviously, the word of Barnabas was trusted because Saul was now welcomed into the fellowship at Jerusalem.

This part of our lesson ends with an important summary verse (9:31) that tells of the expansion of the Church throughout Judea, Galilee, and Samaria. And it also indicates that the Christian believers were "at rest," enjoying a time of peace and blessing "in the comfort of the Holy Ghost." After the fast-paced events of this part of our lesson, it is heartening to know that there may come periods of calm.

The Gospel for Everyone (9:32–11:30)

Luke now suddenly shifts characters. Peter returns to center stage, and we read that he was traveling from place to place preaching the gospel of salvation through faith in Jesus Christ to the Jews (9:32). We have already seen through the ministry of Philip and Saul (Paul) that the Good News was being well received. Up to now, however, the strategy of the Christians had been to win converts from Judaism. But in this part of our lesson a new thrust emerges—gentiles, as well, are seen to be recipients of the gospel. The glorious gospel not only reaches unlikely people (i.e., Saul), but it also penetrates unlikely cultures and races. In fact, we see from this part of the story that the word *unlikely* is erased from the Christian dictionary. For us, of course, over 1,900 years later, there is nothing unlikely or unusual about the idea that the gospel of Jesus recognizes no social, racial, or geographic boundaries. But in those early morning hours of the Christian movement, it was still thought to be only for Jews, wherever they lived.

Peter in Lydda and Joppa.

We pick up Peter now as he "came down also to the saints which dwelt at Lydda" (9:32)—a town west and slightly north of Jerusalem on the road to the seacoast and the port of Joppa. Here we see Peter acting in Jesus' name as he is instrumental in the healing of a palsied man by the name of Aeneas (9:33).

As we might expect, word of this healing got around—even to Joppa on the coast. So we read next that when a Christian in Joppa named Tabitha (Dorcas in Greek) died, her fellow Christians asked Peter "to come to them" (9:36–38). In response to their request, Peter left Lydda and traveled the ten miles to Joppa, where, after he prayed, life was restored to Tabitha (9:40–41).

I believe that Peter's ministry in these two cities was, in a sense, preparatory for the next major event in his life and ministry. But, first, there are two things in the Lydda and Joppa stories that I want to highlight. First, you will notice that Luke uses the word *saints* to describe both the believers in Lydda (vs. 32) and those in Joppa (vs. 41). This word comes from a Greek word that means "different." In other words, the Christians, the saints, were different in belief and behavior from the non-Christians. Now, as then, we are to be a "different people"—in this world, but not of it.

Second, we see in these two stories that God continues to be able and willing to meet the needs of people and of His Church. The miracles performed in these two stories were vehicles by which others came to believe in Christ. But it is important to notice that Peter was not on some sort of a miracle bandwagon. He wasn't engaged in a traveling miracle show. The miracles simply occurred in the natural course of his ministry, and those who saw what happened were convinced of the authenticity of Christianity.

For Peter personally, I believe these events were necessary as a further reminder of the sovereign ability of God to do whatever He chooses. The restoration of life to Tabitha revealed a God who can overrule even death itself. And I believe Peter's ongoing realization that "God can do whatever He wants to do" was essential in preparing him for the series of events that were soon to come in this next part of our lesson.

Once again Luke gives us an abrupt shift of scene. Some thirty-five miles north of Joppa was the thriving port city of Caesarea, the seat of the Roman government in Palestine. Now a new character moves into the Christian drama: "There was a certain man in Caesarea called Cornelius, a centurion of the band called the Italian band" (10:1).

Cornelius, we are told, was a devout man—a man who abandoned a belief in polytheism and was searching for the true God. Luke tells us that he "prayed to God alway" (10:2)—he was already a man of prayer. And it was while he was praying one day that an angel appeared to him, affirmed his prayers and good works, and instructed him

Introducing Cornelius the Centurion.

53

to make contact with Peter, who at that moment was just a few miles south in Joppa. Cornelius then dispatched two servants and an aide to find Peter (10:2–9).

Peter's Vision.   Act two in this drama opens with Peter at noon prayer. First, God had been in communication with Cornelius; now He is working on Peter through a vision (10:9–17). With his keen descriptive sense Luke takes us into the scene—Peter sees what appears to be a sheet coming down from heaven, and in it "were all manner of four-footed beasts...and creeping things, and fowls of the air" (10:12). Then a voice told him to kill and eat. Peter was horrified—he still adhered to the dietary restrictions of Judaism. In spite of the fact that the voice from heaven assured him that in God's sight nothing was unclean, Peter did not respond. The scene was repeated twice more before it disappeared, but he still failed to understand (10:17).

God's timing, though, is always so right. For while Peter was pondering what had happened, the three messengers from Cornelius arrived and told him all about the angel's visit to Cornelius. Peter then fed them and put them up for the night while he made preparations to go with them to Caesarea.

As I reflect on these two scenes, I am struck again by the fact that God initiated this new and essential phase of the universal mission of the gospel with two men—Cornelius and Peter—who were devoted to prayer. Earlier, Luke gave us the example of Ananias, another prayerful man who was trusted with an important mission. We learn from this, I believe, that the deep and significant things of God are for those who spend time in prayer.

You may remember the arrogant and senseless statement of the Soviet astronaut who said that he hadn't seen God anywhere during the time he was in space. In response a Russian Orthodox priest wisely said that we shouldn't be surprised that the astronaut failed to see God in space: "You cannot expect someone to see God in space who has not first seen Him on earth."

Neither could we expect the disciples to be in a position to see, hear, and try such radical new ideas unless they had first established deep and meaningful connections with the Spirit of God. And in the context of the rest of the story, we know that through Peter's prayer and his vision he was uniquely prepared for this drastic new step. His doubts were erased with the appearance of the messengers from Cornelius and the words of the Holy Spirit: "... go with them, doubting nothing: for I have sent them" (10:20).

God had spoken. In fact, He had to speak more than once to Peter through the vision. But that didn't matter. The important thing was that now Peter obeyed. And what matters most for us is that we obey God, for His will and purposes are accomplished by people who obey Him.

The Conversion of Cornelius and His Household.

Next we travel with Peter to Caesarea and to the home of Cornelius. And here comes the proof that Peter finally un-

The port of Caesarea was located between 65 and 70 miles from Jerusalem on the great highway between Tyre and Egypt.

derstood what God had been trying to tell him: "Ye know how that it is an unlawful thing for a man that is a Jew to keep company, or come unto one of another nation; but God hath showed me that I should not call any man common or unclean" (10:28).

With that introduction Luke gives us a full account of what happened (10:24–48). The seeker is reached by the obedient disciple, and this is followed by a clear presentation of the message of salvation through Christ and the attentiveness of Cornelius and his household. And right in the middle of this scene, the Holy Spirit came—just as He had come to the believers on the Day of Pentecost. For the hearers, it was the fulfillment of their desire to know God more fully. For Peter, it was proof positive that "God is no respecter of persons: "But in every nation he that feareth him, and worketh righteousness, is accepted with him" (10:34–35).

This message is relevant today. Inside the Christian Church there is still a spirit of exclusiveness that rears its ugly head and insists that "different people" or people with different ideas are not prime candidates for "our group." To be sure, we would deny this most of the time, but we confirm it by our actions and attitudes. We need to be reminded daily that God is *still* no respecter of persons.

Peter's Defense.   We see just how difficult it was for those early Jewish Christians to understand what was happening in this next part of our lesson (11:1–18). When word of what had happened at Caesarea got back to the Jewish Christians in Jerusalem, they really got nervous. So when Peter returned, they held him to account. Peter had broken the sacred traditions by eating with an uncircumcised gentile. And at this point we must remember that the early Christians, all of whom were Jews or Jewish converts, still tended to understand their new faith in Jesus in terms of their ancestral faith.

The "circumcision group" just couldn't believe that Peter would dare go to those who were uncircumcised. By their standards, even though Cornelius feared God, he was not a candidate for salvation. But to emphasize the importance of this whole issue Luke goes into considerable detail here. Peter rehearsed the entire sequence of events at Joppa and at Caesarea, and then in telling how

Ruins at Caesarea, the home city of Cornelius the centurion to whom Peter preached the gospel.

the Holy Spirit came to the household of Cornelius, he recalled for them the words of Jesus: "John indeed baptized with water; but ye shall be baptized with the Holy Ghost" (11:16).

We have in Peter's defense here a straightforward plea for understanding—a presentation of truth. And it was accepted as such, for Luke now writes, "When they heard these things, they held their peace, and glorified God, saying, Then hath God also to the Gentiles granted repentance unto life" (11:18).

The rest of Acts 11 gives us two other lessons on the theme that the gospel of Jesus is for everyone. First, we see ***The Church at Antioch.***

57

further confirmation of the fact that gentiles were to be included in God's new fellowship of believers (11:19–26).

As the scene shifts to the metropolis of Antioch, we find that not only was the gospel preached there but it was well received. This was most significant since Antioch ranked with Alexandria and Rome in importance in the then-known world. It was a major center of culture and of pagan worship of the goddess Daphne. Antioch was also known as a center of immorality, but it was here that the gospel took firm root and where believers were first called Christians (11:26).

One in Spirit.

The second lesson that comes to us now has to do with the intense connection that existed among the believers (11:27–30). They cared for and about each other. This is illustrated by the visit of Agabus to Antioch. When he told the Christians there about the threatened famine in Judea, they immediately banded together and provided generous relief. They were one in the Spirit and one in the Lord. The wall between Jew and gentile was broken down. Christianity was on the verge of becoming a world religion.

I believe the important lesson for us here is to know that while the gospel is inclusive, it does not gloss over immorality or indecent behavior. But it does include *everyone* who repents of sin, accepts Jesus Christ as Saviour and Lord, and lives consistently with that commitment. For all of these "...old things are passed away; behold, all things are become new" (2 Cor. 5:17). When Jesus is Lord, Christians are forbidden to keep looking in the rear-view mirror!

Growing Pains (12:1–12:25)

The Death of James and Peter's Arrest.

The statement, "The blood of martyrs is the seed of the church" is certainly confirmed in Acts 12. To please the Jewish religious leaders Herod Agrippa launched an attack on the Christian community in Jerusalem: "... he killed James, the brother of John with the sword" (12:2) and he threw Peter into prison (12:3). The period of calm referred to in 9:31 was over, and a campaign of intense persecution was leveled against the Christians.

But in the midst of this time of testing we catch something of the mood of the Church: "Peter therefore was kept in prison: but *prayer was made without ceasing* of the church unto God for him" (12:5, italics mine). In times of difficulty, stress, and persecution, victory comes through prayer.

This is not pious sentimentalism; it is raw truth. Up to this point in our lesson we've seen prayer as the vehicle for service and ministry. Now we see it as the means to deliver and defend Christianity against its enemies.

But prayer should never be interpreted as sort of a magic "cure-all." It is not a divine vending machine into which we drop requests and get back answers. Rather, prayer is communion with God that strengthens us in our faith whether at the moment the results are what we expected or not. In the face of evil, prayer will help us rise above our difficulties and suffering to see the God who is still with us.

In Peter's case, the church prayed and a miracle occurred (12:6–11)—an angel of the Lord freed Peter and led him out to the street. When he appeared at the locked door where the Christians were praying for him, it created quite a commotion. The girl Rhoda answered the door and recognized Peter, but she was so surprised that she forgot to let him in and slammed the door shut as she ran to tell the others that Peter was outside. But they refused to believe her (12:15)—even though they had been praying for Peter, they evidently hadn't expected this kind of an answer. So Peter had to keep knocking until they finally opened up for him. There's a twist of humor in this scene, but so often we're like those Christians that night—we pray and then we're "astonished" when the Lord answers.

Peter Delivered.

God was making an important point here for those early Christians—prison bars, evil plots, and even murder cannot stop the movement of the faith. Luke underlines this in these significant words: "... the word of God grew and multiplied" (12:24).

Christianity had now moved out beyond Judea and Samaria. This is a vivid story of the expansion of faith in Jesus Christ. It is true it didn't happen without problems, perversions, and persecution. But there was no attitude of defeat among these early believers. In fact our Scripture lesson closes with the word that Saul (Paul) and Barnabas and young John Mark were getting ready to leave on what we commonly refer to as Paul's first missionary journey.

In our lesson we have seen that unlikely people, unlikely races, and unlikely circumstances all came together to show us a Christianity on the move. All of this causes me to pray that God will do something unlikely *with* and for me. Who knows what adventures of faith may lay out ahead of us as we commit our lives to the Lord and pray "without ceasing" for His guidance.

I'm so privileged to study Your Word. I appreciate being able to learn about You. AMEN.

WHAT THIS SCRIPTURE MEANS TO ME—Acts 8:4–12:25

He was the last person we thought would darken the door of a church. But much to our amazement we saw him there one Wednesday night with his latest girlfriend. We could tell from the look on his face that he'd rather be anywhere else but in a church youth group meeting.

I remember telling my friends that night that I wouldn't give him more than two weeks before he'd break up with this girlfriend. Then he would be back on the streets, running with his tough crowd again and tossing empty beer bottles at passing automobiles.

Perhaps this shows how little I knew of the startling and undefinable power of God; the power that can completely transform the most unlikely of lives. For later that year, at a summer Young Life camp in upstate New York, this street-wise tough was nearly in tears as he told how God changed his life.

Some of the main characters in our Scripture lesson were about as unlikely candidates for the message of salvation as this young man was. There was Simon the Sorcerer—a man in love with himself and his actions; the Ethiopian eunuch, who had never even heard of the name of Jesus until Philip talked with him on the Gaza road; and Cornelius, a devout man but a soldier of an occupation force. Then, of course, we meet a man named Saul. He went around persecuting people that didn't believe the way he thought they should. This is a strange mixture of people, but they were all brought to one mind by the message of Jesus Christ.

We have seen, beginning with His own disciples, how Jesus' message can unite different kinds of people. Among the Twelve was Simon, a religious zealot, whose life centered on a military overthrow of the Roman government. Then there was Matthew, a tax collector—the most hated symbol of the despised government.

Simon would have killed Matthew in a second had they met in a dark alley. But in the presence of Jesus, they were a living testimony to the good news that people who hate can learn to love each other when they both love Jesus Christ. Lives focused on Christ bring peace, even where there is no peace.

Few men have captured the imagination of world Christians like Bishop Desmond Tutu, Nobel Peace Prize winner and churchman from South Africa. In spite of oppression Bishop Tutu continues to preach the message in his racially divided country that Jesus Christ is *Lord of all*—that everyone, irrespective of color, is equal in God's sight. As a part of a group meeting with him one night in New York, I heard him ask how it was possible to have peace in the world if we all could not live together under God as one people.

In a world rocked with fear and hate, there is a power that reaches not only the hardest of hearts, or even the most shattered of spirits, but it brings about a startling reconciliation among all kinds of people. Saul of Tarsus discovered that transforming power on the Damascus road as he was confronted by the risen Christ. And this same power is available to us in our world today.

On my way to work on the bus one day I heard two men discussing world conditions. In their conversation they expressed concern over a failing economy, crime, and nuclear war. It was rather a dismal picture, but after a time, one man paused for a moment, looked out at the old, grey buildings we were passing, and said, "Ah, but we also believe there is hope. Don't we?"

The other man nodded, and quietly, so did I. We all live in hope—hope in the power of God to change the hearts and lives of people, even the Sauls of the world. It is this hope and power that can bring us together as children of God—in His peace.

LESSON 4
ACTS 13:1—15:35

Establishing the Pattern

Saviour, Help me to establish only those patterns in my life that glorify and please You. AMEN.

In Bill Cosby's classic comedy routine entitled "Noah," God is telling Noah to build an ark. For a moment there is silence. Then Noah responds, "What's an ark?"

When I read the opening verses of our Scripture lesson and see how God is leading the fledgling Christians to be missionary minded, I can almost hear them ask, "What's a missionary?"

As we move in now and participate in the events of this lesson, we will begin to discover an answer to that question through the eyes of those who served as the first missionaries of the Christian faith. For in Acts 13 and 14 we have the story of Paul's first missionary journey.

Keeping in mind the outline which Acts 1:8 provides for us— "...ye shall be witnesses unto me both in Jerusalem [1], and in all Judea, and in Samaria [2], and unto the uttermost part of the earth" [3]—we are now entering the third major division of that commission. The faith has been established in Jerusalem and in Judea and Samaria. From this point on we will see how it develops "unto the uttermost part of the earth." And in this lesson we will examine the establishment of the basic apostolic pattern for expanding the outreach of the Christian gospel.

At the very beginning of our lesson (13:1–3), Luke makes it plain that the basis for Christian outreach is the local congregation of believers. In fact, the book of Acts knows nothing of personal evangelism or church growth apart from the fellowship within the church. And behind every individual witnessing outreach is the presence of a praying and supporting group. The church at Antioch of Syria was just such a church. And as we read the opening verses of our Scripture lesson, it isn't the least bit surprising that God chose this vigorous congregation to launch Christ's mission into all the world. Luke writes: "As they ministered to the Lord, and fasted, the Holy Ghost said, Separate me Barnabas and Saul for the work whereunto I have called them. And when they had fasted and prayed, and laid their hands on them, they sent them away" (13:2–3).

I believe it will help us in our own growth and spiritual development to take a close look at the character of those

Paul's First Missionary Journey (13-14)

The Sending Church.

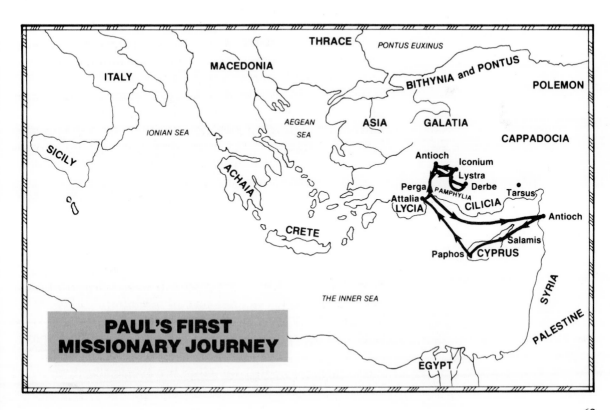

PAUL'S FIRST MISSIONARY JOURNEY

Antioch Christians and the qualities of the church that set apart and sponsored the first missionary efforts of Paul and Barnabas.

First, the church was made up of a reputable congregation of believers. Remember, Antioch of Syria was a bustling, pagan metropolis, but it was here that the title "Christian" was given to followers of Christ. The genuineness of their faith and life showed that they had been with Jesus. From that base of solid believability the world outreach of Christianity could grow.

It is amazing how interconnected our witness and our reputations are. If as Christians our words and our actions don't match, our influence and our witness become tarnished and not believable. This is true in the neighborhoods and towns in which we live, and it is equally true on a national and international scale. For many years the Western world has been the leader in missionary outreach and world evangelism. But as the moral fiber of Western society has become soft, Third World nations are beginning to assume spiritual leadership and in some cases are sending missionaries to countries that once evangelized them. To have power, our witness must be reputable.

A second quality that distinguished the Antioch church was its *diverse* congregation. The believers were involved with a diversity of ministries. Two ministries are mentioned especially in verse 1: prophecy and teaching. Teachers were involved in training and nurturing their fellow Christians in the churches. On the other hand, the prophets traveled across the countryside preaching God's Word and seeking converts. It was this diversity of gifts and abilities that enabled them to be effective Christians.

We notice also that they were racially diverse. Five persons who were apparently in leadership positions are mentioned (13:1). Simeon called Niger was probably black and from Africa, and Lucius was from Cyrene, also in Africa. Saul was, of course, a Jew from Tarsus in Cilicia, and Barnabas was a Jew from Cyprus. It seems clear from this brief mention that neither race nor geographical location was a barrier to inclusion in the church of Antioch. This in itself certainly set an international mood so important to a missionary vision.

We know, too, that the church was socially diverse. It seems likely that Barnabas and Simeon were not persons of high social standing. On the other hand, Manaen apparently had connections in high social and political circles because of Luke's careful mention of his connection with Herod. And we have every reason to believe that Paul's family was evidently prominent in Tarsus. Just this brief mention would seem to indicate both a socially diverse and a socially inclusive congregation. There is a vitality to this kind of atmosphere that is lacking when everyone in any group seems to be cut from the same mold. The Christians in Antioch had their priorities straight—they weren't going out to establish churches with any particular kind of social ranking. Their vision was to expand the body of Christ.

And finally, we know that the Antioch church had a worshipful congregation (13:2–3). They fasted and prayed, and it was in this attitude of worship that the Lord was able to speak to them about Barnabas and Paul. We can only speculate as to whether or not this call would or could have come had they not been devoted to worship, prayer, and fasting. I doubt it. And I further suspect that many Christians and churches miss their "word from the Lord" because they are not committed to worship.

We know, too, that at Antioch worship was not perfunctory, for Luke says, "they ministered to the Lord." The word *ministered* in Greek expresses *acts of devoted service*. In other words, when they worshiped God, they offered themselves completely to Him. Apparently, worship was not a passive act for them; it required instead an active involvement.

This brings us now to the fourth quality that distinguished the church at Antioch. They were a *responsive* group of Christians. Paul and Barnabas had been central figures in the founding of the church. Consequently, it would have been easy for the members to want to keep them there in ongoing leadership. This is our attitude so often. We tend to focus on the capabilities and personality of the pastor—everything is planned and built around him or her. But at Antioch it was different. They didn't identify the life of their church with any person or group. They were not locked into any person for success. This gave them the freedom to openly respond to God's voice when He spoke to them.

There is so much for us to reflect upon in the opening

three verses of this lesson, and we can learn a great deal from these first-century Syrian Christians. They have given us a model of integrity in words and actions, a pattern for unity in diversity, and an awareness of the vitality of worship.

Beyond Magic.

Following their commissioning by the Antioch Christians, Paul and Barnabas, accompanied by young John Mark, took a ship at Seleucia, the seaport for Antioch, and sailed to Cyprus, Barnabas's homeland. Their first stop was at the port city of Salamis on the east end of the island (13:5). After delivering their message of Good News there, they traveled west across the rugged country to Paphos, a seaport city at the west end of the island and headquarters for the Roman government there. Here, two interesting characters enter the scene: Sergius Paulus, the Roman proconsul, and a magician named Elymas (13:5–12).

As the drama unfolds, it becomes clear that Sergius Paulus was open to the gospel message, even though Paphos, as a city, was devoted to the worship of Venus. But Elymas, the magician, attempted to divert the proconsul's interest. He knew that if Sergius Paulus became a Christian, his influence as a magician-sorcerer would be over. Out of the many things that happened on Cyprus, Luke chose to highlight this event. We can only speculate what his reason was, but I believe he wanted to build a case against the evil and destructive deception involved in the kind of magic Elymas practiced

When I speak of magic here, I'm not referring to the harmless sleight-of-hand tricks and illusions that are performed for the amusement of an audience. Elymas practiced a sinister kind of magic and fortune-telling, one that perverted "the right ways of the Lord" (13:10). In effect, Elymas had Sergius Paulus "under his spell," and, of course, anything that would remove that spell was a threat.

Paul, Luke tells us, was equal to the test and, inspired by the Holy Spirit, castigated Elymas publicly and declared that he would be blind for a time (13:10–11). When Sergius Paulus saw the power of the Holy Spirit acting through Paul, he became a believer in Jesus Christ.

From our perspective, how do we apply this episode to our own lives? I believe that in this episode we have an object lesson on the necessity of moving beyond any and

Ruins at Salamis on the island of Cyprus, the first port of call for Paul and Barnabas on their first missionary journey.

all false illusions that can blind us to reality. We are to move beyond reliance on self or dependency on anything or anyone. Any dependency—except on God—is an illusion that is tragically deceptive.

Thomas Merton, through his writings, has helped me wrestle with this truth. While Merton welcomed anything that promoted genuine human progress, he knew certain things that might appear to be progress were not and would actually retard it, especially if and when we come to depend on them for ultimate meaning. Merton urges us to think seriously about the illusions that are created by technology, mass media, racism, violence, and what he called "mass man" (i.e., the loss of individuality at the expense of image). All of these point to the primary illusion—that we are sufficient unto ourselves for life.

We live in a time of wonders. If our great-great-grandparents could visit our world today, they would think they had stepped into a magic kingdom—television, microwave ovens, walking on the moon, space travel, organ transplants. In all the wonders of modern life there is the subtle temptation to give in to the illusion of being our own gods. But the message of Paul and Barnabas and John Mark on Cyprus a little over 1,900 years ago, that only through Jesus Christ do we find reality and meaning, is our up-to-date answer for today.

Beyond Tradition. The move beyond magic takes us past the limits of secularized world views about the meaning of life. The move beyond tradition, which we will consider now, transcends the limits of religion, narrowly understood. This section of Acts (13:13–52) pictures graphically how difficult that is. Just as Elymas opposed the move beyond magic, the Jews in Pisidian Antioch opposed the move beyond tradition.

Dietrich Bonhoeffer was one of the first theologians to speak of "religionless Christianity." When I take his writings as a whole, I do not believe he was suggesting an expression of the faith that is religionless or anti-religious. Rather, I believe he was calling for the church to move beyond the limits of its perspective (no matter how well-intentioned or sincerely held) to embrace a bigger view of Christianity than ever before. This is precisely what Paul and Barnabas were doing when they moved into Antioch in Pisidia.

Before going on, though, let's pick up on their travels. When their mission in Paphos on Cyprus was completed, the three travelers sailed northwest to Perga in the province of Pamphylia, located on the south coast of Asia Minor. It was here that John Mark abruptly left Paul and Barnabas and headed for home. We don't know what went wrong, but we do know there was ill feeling because of what happened at the beginning of Paul's second missionary journey.

From the port city of Perga, Paul and Barnabas set out for Antioch in Pisidia. Their journey of approximately 160 miles called for them to make their way over rugged country from sea level to an altitude of over 3,500 feet to Antioch on the other side of the Taurus mountains. It is likely they arrived there in the late summer of A.D. 45–46.

The scene in Antioch opens with Paul and Barnabas in the synagogue, where, after the reading of the Scriptures, they were invited to speak. The scene continues then to the next Sabbath day when crowds gathered in huge numbers to hear Paul again, and the Jewish leaders became envious of their popularity. We see in this part of our lesson that the *move beyond tradition is first from within* (13:13–46). In the major part of this section Luke gives us Paul's address that first Sabbath day in the synagogue. Here we have a marvelous example of his preaching.

In the sermon we see how Paul attempts to move his listeners beyond their tradition from within it. He traces how God had "moved" the Jews along from the time of their being chosen by God as His special people, throughout their 400 years of slavery and oppression in Egypt, their exodus and years in the wilderness, to their entry into the Promised Land. He then shows how God had "moved" them from being led by judges and prophets to being ruled by kings. And he climaxes his sermon by indicating that King David himself pointed to the coming of Jesus Christ. Paul had given them an excellent lesson on their religious roots, and it was evidently well received.

Such reviews of our faith are helpful, and even necessary, if we are to see things in perspective and get a vision for the next step in our Christian development. This is why so many of the teachings and sermons found in our Bible include the recounting of past events. A "memory" of the past is essential to understanding both the present and the future. As we "connect" with our tradition, we are given a sense of continuity with the actions of God in times past. And at the same time we are better able to understand the present implications of our tradition.

I believe, for example, that it is important for each of us to understand our spiritual heritage. I'll illustrate this with my own background. I am part of the Wesleyan tradition in my faith and practice. As I have reflected on the historical development of that tradition, I have been reminded of the importance of the life of holiness. This has caused me to take a deeper look at Christian discipline in a larger sense. But even as I've "connected" with that tradition, I've been challenged to *move within it* to take the next step—social holiness. I'm seeing the necessity of extending "holy living" beyond the personal to my relationship with and responsibility to others. This represents my move beyond tradition from within.

I suspect that you will also benefit from a thoughtful recollection of your own Christian tradition. An understanding of where you are and where you came from will position you in a community of believers in which you are comfortable and feel at home. And you may discover aspects of your background and tradition that will move you beyond where you are now even as you remain true to your heritage. This can be a very exciting pilgrimage toward Christian maturity.

Paul's message was clear that day in the synagogue. Everything within the tradition of his listeners focused on the coming of Jesus Christ and culminated in His death and resurrection. We find a marked similarity between Paul's sermon here and that of Peter's on the Day of Pentecost (Acts 2). The challenge is to build on the past, acknowledge that Jesus Christ was the fulfillment of their history, and move ahead into the future under the leadership of the Holy Spirit.

We come now to that second Sabbath day in Antioch. While large crowds gathered to hear Paul, the Jewish leaders, envious of his popularity, began to spread dissension and accused him of blasphemy. It was then that Paul exploded a bombshell with the word that the move beyond tradition is not only from within, but *from without* (13:46–52). They had to believe that God was just as willing to offer Christ to the gentile as to the Jew. And Paul made it clear that their instructions from the Lord were to be a "light of the Gentiles, that thou shouldest be for salvation unto the ends of the earth" (13:47). Naturally, when the gentiles in the crowd heard this, they were delighted and many believed, but the Jews were angry and incited the crowd to opposition and persecution.

The *move from without* in this case called for the Jew to

accept the gentile. It leads us, I believe, to a spirit of mutual love and cooperation with our Christian brothers and sisters who are a part of traditions that differ from ours. Our tendency to be critical of any and all who don't dot the "i" and cross the "t" just the way we do seems to go against the prayer of Jesus for unity in John 17. Later, Paul expressed it well when he wrote, "There is neither Jew nor Greek, there is neither bond nor free, there is neither male nor female: for ye are all one in Christ Jesus" (Gal. 3:28). The gospel flame had been lit. It had spread from Jerusalem into Judea and Samaria. Now, it had cut a path into the heart of Asia Minor—Pisidian Antioch in what is now central Turkey.

Beyond Praise and Persecution.

Recently I attended the commissioning service for about a hundred students who will be serving in various capacities through our seminary-supervised ministries program. When they were asked to stand for the dedicatory prayer, it was a moving sight. As I prayed for them, I realized that some were in for joyous and profitable experiences. Others would experience frustration and heartache. But on that day they stood together, united in their commitment to serve the Lord in their assigned places.

When Paul and Barnabas moved out on this first missionary journey, they had no idea what the response to their efforts would be. They knew what we must know— there are no guarantees. Chapter 14 of Acts shows us that we must move beyond a dependence on praise or fear of persecution in our life and service for God.

When Paul and Barnabas left Antioch, they traveled southeast about ninety miles on the Roman road to the ancient city of Iconium. Here as before, the two missionaries boldly proclaimed the message of salvation (14:1), and while many believed, those who did not, set out to make trouble. Paul and Barnabas nevertheless stood firm and it is thought that they stayed on in Iconium for the entire winter.

Remaining in Iconium in spite of opposition and persecution was a vital necessity for the confirmation of the new believers. Paul and Barnabas knew that the new Christians were far from established in their faith. Had they not stuck by them, they might have been lost to the opposition. This is an important truth for us to remember in our own experience. <u>Our task is not only to point others to Christ, but also to stand by and with them as they move toward maturity. We need to be cautious about hit-and-run witnessing.</u>

I think, also, that staying in Iconium was vitally important for Paul and Barnabas in their confrontation with the paganism of the Graeco-Roman world and its sophisticated culture. This called not only for warmhearted witnessing and preaching, but also for hardheaded debate. As Christianity moved into this arena, it was forced to interact with long-standing philosophical, religious, and political value systems. Only those who were prepared to become engaged in dialogue with those systems could ever hope to sway men and women from them. This is why it is important that we not withdraw or insulate ourselves from society and culture if our witness is to be understood and have credibility.

Paul and Barnabas were obviously well-suited for their task. Paul's background and training both in Tarsus and in Jerusalem had ably prepared him for dialogue with the intelligentsia in the Greek and Roman world. His early training served him well as a Christian communicator. And we learn from this the importance of our being well trained for our role of living out our Christian faith in the complex world of today. Competent, trained ministers and lay persons are essential to the movement of the Good News into our world. This is precisely why the kind of Bible study we're involved in here is so important—as we know and understand our faith, we become better witnesses for the Lord.

But, finally, the opposition in Iconium became too strong. The mobs got violent and threatened a lynching, so Paul and Barnabas traveled southwest from Iconium to Lystra, about a six-hour trip. Luke then explains that they preached the gospel there, in nearby Derbe and the surrounding area. It was here that Paul and Barnabas confronted a different kind of a problem (14:8–18). And in this episode we learn that the base for our service to the Lord is not in *praise* received.

When Paul healed the man in Lystra who had been crippled since birth, he unwittingly unleashed a wave of emotion that soon got out of hand. The people of Lystra were immersed in Roman and Greek mythology, and they immediately interpreted the healing as being done by Jupiter and Mercurius, or Zeus and Hermes in Greek lore (14:12). And Luke then tells us that the priest of Jupiter made preparation to offer sacrifices to them (14:13). It is significant that Paul and Barnabas stood as firmly against this false praise as they had against the fierce persecution in Iconium.

Paul's reaction to what had happened is interesting. Luke writes that he and Barnabas tore their clothes and ran around among the people, shouting, "We also are men of like passions with you" (14:15). They tried desperately to show their humanity. Their confidence in the gospel was so great that they knew this exposure of their humanness would not detract from it.

Paul and Barnabas were realists. Their actions here remind us that real people are Christ's best witnesses. The Incarnation of Jesus reminds us that humanity is an acceptable "package" for transmitting the gospel message. And when we realize that, we are free to do what Paul and Barnabas did—concentrate on the message, not on ourselves (14:15–17).

And it is the message that Jesus Christ came to give us New Life that counts. It isn't the personality or the looks of the messenger that makes the difference. Religious sideshows are not the vehicle for relieving the hurts of people. There's no need to jazz up the message. It's as simple now as it was in the first century: "But as many as received him, to them gave he power to become the sons of God, even to them that believe on his name" (John 1:12).

The "high" soon became a low. Some Jews from Antioch and Iconium had possibly heard about what was happening in Lystra. Hurrying there, they were successful in turning the people against Paul. Their former adulation turned to hate. They stoned Paul and left him for dead. But Luke tells us he wasn't dead, and when he revived, he courageously went right back into the city and spent the night there before going on to Derbe (14:20).

After preaching and witnessing in Derbe, Paul and Barnabas then retraced their steps—going first to Lystra, then to Iconium and Antioch. At each stage of the trip they affirmed and encouraged the new Christians who had found the Lord during the missionaries' earlier visit. Finally, they moved south to Perga and then over to Attalia where they took a ship back to Antioch in Syria.

The time involved in this first missionary journey is an estimated three years. The gospel of Jesus had now moved into several Roman outposts in Asia Minor in its march toward the imperial city itself. And throughout the entire trip Paul and Barnabas had remained faithful to their calling in spite of both persecution and unwarranted praise. They had risked much as they sought new converts and nurtured new Christians. The cost had been high, but as Dietrich Bonhoeffer expressed it, "When Christ calls a man, he bids him come and die."

The Jerusalem Council (15:1–35)

The Winchester House in San Jose, California, is a regular stop for tour buses. Many years ago, as the story goes, Mrs. Winchester had the peculiar notion that she wouldn't die as long as she kept building on and adding rooms to her house. Rooms were added willy-nilly, and to the rooms were added fake passageways and false staircases. Naturally, the house lacks continuity, design, and focus. It serves as a grim reminder of what can happen when reality is exchanged for fanaticism.

In our study of Acts so far we have observed a church growing rapidly and in diverse settings. If we could step back and view the scene from a distance, we might see something akin to the Winchester House. The close-up design might not seem clear, and certainly, the rapid growth was not without its problems.

Trouble in Antioch.

When Paul and Barnabas returned to the church in Antioch, Syria, they found it in turmoil. A deputation of Jewish Christians had arrived there from Judea and had declared, "Except ye be circumcised after the manner of Moses, ye cannot be saved" (15:1). In other words, the gentile Christians had to become Jews or they couldn't be saved. Obviously, these Jerusalem Jews were among those who viewed Christianity as nothing more than a Jewish sect. Old ways of thinking and believing die hard—certainly some beliefs had not died at all.

So, with the grand success of their first missionary tour just barely behind them, Paul and Barnabas and the rest of the Christians in Antioch had to wrestle with their most critical problem yet. When the issue couldn't be settled locally, it was "determined that Paul and Barnabas, and certain other of them, should go up to Jerusalem unto the apostles and elders about this question" (15:2). The question was critical: Was the gospel for a few Jews or was it for everyone?

And so we have the setting for what has since been referred to as the First Church Council or the Apostolic Council, which met in Jerusalem in A.D. 49.

The Council in Session.

The apostles and elders gathered in a formal meeting. Of primary importance is that they started off by allowing *a full airing of opinion*. Earlier Paul and Barnabas had given a full report on their trip and on the dispute in Antioch. Then Peter, having learned his lesson well in Joppa and Caesarea, argued against the attempt to Judaize the gentile Christians (15:7–11). Next Paul and Barnabas spoke to the assembly, "...declaring what miracles and wonders God had wrought among the Gentiles by them" (15:12).

There seems to have been no limit placed on the debate. No perspective was given preference over another during the discussion. Also, no assumptions about right and wrong were made prematurely. All involved were Christians, and everyone was given the opportunity to speak his mind. The atmosphere was charged because of the importance of the issue.

Following the discussion the group *looked to trusted leaders to bring perspective*. Then after Peter and Paul and Barnabas were heard, James, the acknowledged leader of the church in Jerusalem, spoke (15:13–21). The atmosphere was one of quiet and respectful attentiveness. The issue was momentous.

As James spoke, it became clear that *the Scriptures were the final court of appeal*. Even though the witness of the respected apostles seemed conclusive, no decision was made without confirmation from the Old Testament. The prophecy of Amos (9:11–12) served as the ultimate voice. Through it the prophet spoke of the restoration of Israel, but did so not in terms of the Jews alone, but also of the gentiles.

I am deeply impressed with the sequence of events in this meeting. First, all opinions were heard. Then came the perspective of the mature leaders, and under the guidance of James the authority of the Scriptures was invoked. Finally, James offered the solution. The gentile Christians would not be required to take on the traditions of Judaism. But in order to make it possible for Jew and gentile to experience fellowship together without social strain, the gentiles were asked to avoid idol contamination of any kind, to not practice fornication, and to eat nothing that had been strangled and from which the blood had not been drained (in other words, their meat was to be prepared according to Jewish custom). By following these simple and reasonable rules, Jew and gentile Christians could associate together without offending each other.

Antioch Christians Reassured.

Now we come to the final act in the Church Council drama. *The decision was clearly communicated* (15:22–31). It was to be written down carefully and entrusted to Judas and Silas, who were to accompany Paul and Barnabas and deliver it in person to the Christians in Syrian Antioch. The key words here, I believe, are, "...it seemed good to the Holy Ghost, and to us..." (15:28). Here we see the coming together of divine and human wills. That alone could have produced the spirit of "one accord" (15:25), which ultimately came to characterize the Jerusalem conference.

Behind all of this is an unspoken but significant fact— there is no mention that anyone was excommunicated from the fellowship. People on both sides of the dispute still appeared to be in the church after the smoke had cleared away. This in itself is a powerful testimony, especially when so many of our disputes today end in division, hard feelings, and losers leaving the church. Too often we start with division and end with schism, but they started with division and ended with unity. We forget too easily that the purpose of decision-making is to strengthen the unity of the church. The early Christians seem to have kept the desire for unity uppermost in the whole process. The final result was a general spirit of encouragement and an underlying spirit of revival (15:31–35).

An interesting "full circle" has occurred in this lesson. We started in Antioch in Syria, and we end there. The church that contained the qualities necessary to be a sending church was also the church that had the qualities necessary to receive and integrate a critical decision. In between the basic pattern in the establishment of the Christian faith was the repeated call of God to "move beyond" those things that would have perpetually hindered the Christians.

There are many questions for us in this lesson. Are we the kind of church that can both send out the gospel in mission and receive it in decision? Have we moved beyond magic, tradition, praise, and persecution? Have we cultivated mature and respected leaders to whom we can look for perspective? Do we accept the Bible as normative in matters of faith and practice, and do we know it well enough to be able to distinguish between a word from the Lord and a proof text?

These are all vital questions to us now, even as they were to first-century Christians. We've come a long way since then, but the principles illuminated in this lesson are still valid today.

The Antioch Church is a splendid example of a Christian fellowship. Thank You for including examples in Your Word that encourage us. AMEN.

WHAT THIS SCRIPTURE MEANS TO ME—
Acts 13:1—15:35

It was a tragedy unlike any that the small rural community had ever seen. The teenage son of the general store owner had been found dead behind the store.

Everyone in town attended the funeral, for the boy was well-liked. He was president of his high school class, played in the band and on the basketball team, and was active at church. Shortly before, the good news had arrived that he had just won a scholarship for the state university. He was the all-American kid, always smiling. Nothing ever seemed to bother him.

When the routine police investigation of the death came up empty, rumors of suicide began to spread throughout the community. And then the note was found. "I thought I always had to be happy," it read, "and that made it too hard to be sad."

"Too hard to be sad." We'll never know the pain that that young man felt in his heart, or why he felt it. He showed the rest of the world only the smiles, the good times; the tears, the pain and hurt had apparently been pressed down deep inside.

Most of us, I'm sure, are often tempted to cover up or hide our "leaning sides."

I find myself wanting to protect my image, one that as a Christian means I must always be tough enough, deep enough in faith, to handle anything. I want to look perfect to my friends and neighbors, even though I know I'm not. It is a strong temptation to gloss over our weaknesses.

I wonder if it was ever tempting for Luke to do the same when he was writing the book of Acts. For example, when Luke was writing about that first great missionary journey of Paul's, was he tempted to cover the slipups with flowery language? It would have been so easy to write a "too-good-to-be-true" victory story that would have claimed an exaggerated account of the number of conversions.

But it didn't happen that way. Instead, Luke called it as he saw it. And he saw events like desertion—John Mark giving up and going home when things got tough. He told about Paul and Barnabas being attacked and run out of town. And he reported bitter words of dissension and disagreement between Paul and other believers. No, all was not well in the early church, not by any stretch of the imagination.

Yet, through it all, Luke also allows us to see the grandeur of the power and workings of God throughout the entire trip. And the message for me is so reassuring: I needn't be perfect for a perfect God to work in and through me.

That's been a hard lesson to learn. I used to think there was no room in my life as a Christian for chinks in the armor, chips in the façade. And so the answer for everyone to "How are you" was always "fine," even when it wasn't. Somehow I feared that people would think less of me if they knew that I'd blown it, that I was down. After all, Christians didn't operate that way. Now, slowly, with the help and support of others, I'm opening up a little, admitting the hurt. It isn't easy. But it helps me to cope with the struggles of life when I know it's okay to struggle. And it's all right for other people to know I struggle, too.

What does this Scripture mean to me? It gives me the glad good news that I don't need to be afraid of being me, to be God's. It's okay to be human.

LESSON 5
ACTS 15:36—18:22

Responding to the Unexpected: Paul's Second Missionary Journey

Redeemer, Open my eyes, my ears, my heart, to receive the truths You have for me in this lesson. AMEN.

One of the greatest testing times in our faith comes when we are confronted by the unexpected. When life falls into neat, predictable patterns, we easily develop a sense of confidence and even control over our lives. However, to do this is to live under an illusion. In fact, life is always unpredictable. We constantly live on the edge of the unexpected and the unknown. How we think and function when we cross over that edge is a matter of great importance in our discipleship.

In this lesson we will watch Paul experience and respond to many unexpected events in his life and ministry. As the lesson opens, it is clear that his intention was to pay a comfortable follow-up visit to those he had previously won and nurtured in the faith (15:36). That decision in itself, plus the events that transpired, brings "the unexpected" clearly into focus.

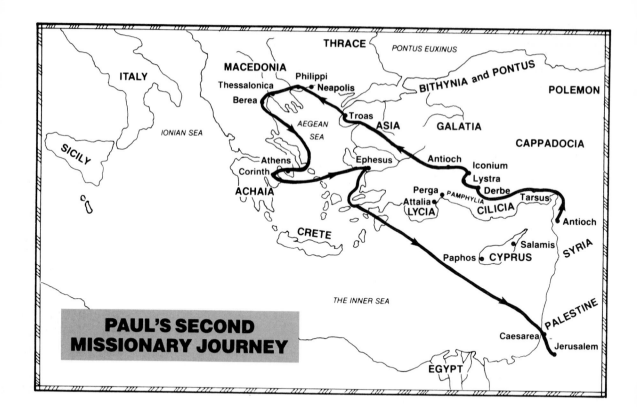

MACEDONIA
Thessalonica   Philippi
Berea   Neapolis

THRACE   PONTUS EUXINUS

ITALY

BITHYNIA and PONTUS

POLEMON

IONIAN SEA

AEGEAN
SEA

Troas   ASIA   GALATIA

CAPPADOCIA

SICILY

Athens   Ephesus   Antioch   Iconium
Corinth   Lystra
ACHAIA   Perga   PAMPHYLIA   Derbe
Attalia   Tarsus
LYCIA   CILICIA

Antioch

CRETE   Salamis   SYRIA
Paphos   CYPRUS

THE INNER SEA

PALESTINE

Caesarea
Jerusalem

**PAUL'S SECOND
MISSIONARY JOURNEY**

EGYPT

**From Antioch to Troas
(15:36–16:10)**

Problems with Partners.

As soon as the Jerusalem Council adjourned, Paul and Barnabas traveled the almost four hundred miles north to Antioch to report the results. And it was here that they faced a great personal crisis. What seemed like the period of greatest unity for them, turned out to be their time of greatest disunity.

As they prepared to embark on their second missionary journey to revisit the churches they had earlier established in Asia Minor, Barnabas wanted to take his nephew John Mark along. Paul refused and they went separate ways, never to labor together again (15:37–41).

Here is probably the most ironic event in the book of Acts. Barnabas was the central figure in Paul's acceptance by the Church after his conversion. Together they formed the "winning combination" in establishing Christianity in the key cities of Syria and Asia Minor. Working in harmony, they had helped overcome a potentially destructive controversy in the Church at the Jerusalem council. If ever there was a "team" in the Christian faith, Paul and Barnabas were it. Yet, their difference of opinion was so strong now that they separated. What does this say to us?

First, it warns us of the danger of living by assumption. John Mark's defection on that first trip didn't seem to have created much controversy at the time it happened (13:13). Perhaps Paul and Barnabas both assumed they had worked through the issue. But ironically, it became the very thing that led to their separation. And in comparison to other events and issues they'd faced, it seemed to be a little thing. But it was the issue now that threatened to disrupt God's work. This happens all too often in our churches today. Frequently, when things appear to be going smoothly, contention and disunity create problems.

Second, it warns us that spiritual victory does not insulate us from spiritual chaos. The church at Antioch was just completing one of its greatest periods of encouragement and revival. Positive attitudes had combined with a spirit of unity to make that period a great time to be a member of that church. Yet, two of their leaders were involved in a dispute. And undoubtedly this caused concern among the believers there. From our vantage point, it is difficult to make a judgment as to who was right or wrong in this case. We do know, though, that in times of intense disagreement and contention among Christians, Satan can easily move in and create havoc.

Third, it reminds us that what may appear to be an initial defeat does not necessarily undo the will of God. Fortunately, this did not happen in this instance. Barnabas took John Mark and returned to Cyprus (15:39). And we have no reason to believe that Barnabas had anything other than a successful ministry on this and subsequent missionary trips. We do know from later references that apparently Barnabas's faith in Mark was justified. And there was even an apparent reconciliation between Paul and Mark, for in 2 Timothy, Paul writes, "Only Luke is with me. Take Mark, and bring him with thee: for he is profitable to me for the ministry" (2 Tim. 4:11).

As we move through this lesson—the account of Paul's second missionary journey, we will see that God blessed his efforts greatly and dramatically. From Antioch Paul and Silas headed north on foot almost 150 miles to Tarsus. And

Paul and Silas Revisit the Churches.

An old Roman road in Syria between Antioch and Aleppo. Roman roads bound together the main cities in the Roman Empire in the time of Paul.

from there they made their way through the rugged and steep pass known as the Cilician Gates that cut across the 7,000 foot high Taurus mountains. Next, they moved west to Derbe and Lystra—probably some 125 to 150 miles from Tarsus. Here Paul and Silas connected with Timothy, a promising young man.

Paul was quite taken with Timothy and selected him as a traveling companion in the Lord. But first, Luke tells us that Paul "took and circumcised him because of the Jews which were in those quarters: for they knew all that his father was a Greek" (16:3). On the surface Paul's action here may seem confusing. After all, hadn't the Jerusalem council settled the entire matter of circumcision?

Yes, it had, but it is important for us to remember that the Jerusalem ruling applied to the gentiles. Timothy was half Jewish. And so I believe the circumcision of Timothy was a witness to two powerful truths, both of which were vitally important in Paul's ministry and to the development of the Christian faith.

First, Paul acknowledged Timothy's "Jewishness" in the act of circumcision and thus legitimized the marriage of his Jewish mother to his Greek father. To the strict Jew this interracial marriage would not have been valid. This would make Timothy a renegade halfbreed. But by circumcising Timothy, Paul demonstrated that he had risen above the narrow interpretation of the Law and that he accepted Timothy's parents now as full participants in God's covenant.

Second, Paul acknowledged the need fo fully integrate Timothy into the heritage of his Jewishness. Had Timothy been a full-blooded gentile, Paul would not have circumcised him. But because he was partly Jewish Paul did not want any occasion to arise among fellow Jews where Timothy's personhood would be questioned.

We might well ask ourselves at this point: what is the practical lesson in all of this for us? I see two things here. First, Paul was completely freed from racial and nationalistic barriers in the expression of the Christian faith—the gospel was indeed for all. At the same time he remained sensitive to the traditions of Jewish life and thought. It is terribly easy for us to become paternalistic and nationalistic in our interpretation of Christianity. But we have in Paul's actions here a model of Christian behavior that rises above man-made barriers and is still sensitive to the feelings of others.

The second thing I see here is the importance of a nurturing ministry. I believe our calling is to be Christian mentors to those around us. In Timothy, Paul saw a promising young person, and he set out to build the young man up in the faith.

Before continuing on I want to underline an interesting

83

thing that has happened here. Paul established the prototype of team ministry on his first missionary journey. With him then were Barnabas and young John Mark. That combination would no longer work. But Paul still apparently believed in team ministry because he now had Silas and young Timothy with him—two people who were to remain close to him for the rest of his life.

Now Luke picks up in the action (16:6–8). The details are sparse, but we know that the three men traveled "throughout Phrygia and the region of Galatia... And they passing by Mysia came down to Troas." This simply means that from Derbe and Lystra, they traveled on to Iconium and Pisidian Antioch and from there headed north and west to Troas (near ancient Troy) on the Aegean seacoast—an overland trip of about 900 miles, probably all covered on foot. This is a long trip across modern Turkey in an automobile. On foot, it must have been a grueling and hazardous journey!

When God Says "No."

Before moving into the dramatic event at Troas, I want to reflect for a moment on another aspect of this lesson. Everything that is written about Paul suggests that he was a man of careful planning. This second missionary trip began with the clear intention of visiting the Christians and the churches where he had been before (15:36). And in the early phases of the trip everything seemed to move along according to plan.

After a time, though, it seems that Paul wanted to take the gospel into a new territory. He wanted to travel to the far northern parts of Asia Minor. Had he done this it would have meant that the Christian gospel would have penetrated as far north as the Black Sea. But Luke tells us that on two occasions his plans were redirected by the Holy Spirit (16:6–7). Instead, Paul was directed west to Troas.

This raises the interesting question of how we should respond when God says "No" to us and our plans. Most of us have had the experience of making plans that we felt sure were right, but then something happened that moved us in a different direction. This has happened to me twice—once in high school and again upon completion of my graduate studies. Both times I was taken in an entirely different direction from what I thought was right for me. Most of us can identify with experiences like that.

And because of this, I see three reasons why this particular experience of Paul's can be helpful to us.

First, there is nothing about this experience that *belittles the fact that Paul had made plans for a certain course of action*. In a very matter-of-fact manner Luke paints a picture for us here of a divinely appointed missionary who tried to do the right thing. I'm sure he had prayed and asked to know God's will for him and his party. And once he felt he had it, he acted. I just believe that God never belittles a person who acts according to the guidance he or she feels has been given.

Second, this part of the lesson makes it clear that *God is sovereign and we are to "sit loose" as we move ahead with our plans*. We don't get any hint in the words of Acts 16:6–8 that Paul and his party were uptight or frustrated. Instead, we see the guidance of the Holy Spirit at work and their acceptance of what is happening. We don't see any indication that Paul tried to force his will on God or manipulate circumstances to get his way.

Third, *we are reminded that God's "No" will lead us to a better "Yes."* At first, Paul's vision had been to cover a small territory, but now in Troas he receives a vision for eastern Europe (16:8–10). God speaks to him through a vision, and he sees a man from Macedonia who says, "Come over into Macedonia and help us" (16:9). This was clearly the voice of God—His "No" to northern Asia Minor was a "Yes" to Europe.

The Gospel in Greece (16:11–18:17)

Heeding the Call.

It was at Troas that Luke joined Paul and Silas and Timothy—there is an interesting shift of pronouns from "they" to "we" in verse 10—"And after he had seen the vision, immediately *we* endeavored to go into Macedonia, assuredly gathering that the Lord had called *us* to preach the gospel unto them" (italics mine). The four men then took a ship, in obedience to the vision, and sailed across the northern part of the Aegean Sea to the port city of Neapolis, modern day Kavalla, a distance of almost 150 miles. And from there they walked inland on the Roman Egnatian Way fifteen miles to the city of Philippi. Philippi was an old and established Roman colony, heavily populated by retired Roman soldiers and their families. Here Paul was to establish his first foothold for the Lord in Europe. Here, too, he was brought into contact with a wide variety of

Neapolis, modern Kavalla, was the port of entry for Philippi. It was at this port that Paul landed on his first visit to Macedonia and Europe.

people—some would respond readily, others would be difficult and contentious. This would be true throughout the entire trip, but Paul's training up to this point had prepared him well.

The First Convert at Philippi.

There were so few Jews in Philippi that there wasn't a synagogue. So on the Sabbath Paul and his companions went down to the river where some Godly inclined people evidently met together. There they met "a certain woman named Lydia, a seller of purple, of the city of Thyatira, which worshipped God." Luke then tells us that she heard Paul's message, was converted, and opened up her home for them to use as their headquarters in Philippi (16:13–15). Luke carefully identifies Lydia with her hometown of Thyatira, a Roman colony in the province of Asia about one hundred miles southeast of Troas. It is possible that some time after this Lydia returned to Thyatira and was one of the founders of the church there.

One of the great joys of Christianity is that it brings us into fellowship with some marvelous people—people who, like Lydia, use hospitality as an effective form of evangelism. It is quite possible that her practice of hospitality was contagious among the growing Christian community of Philippi because some ten years after this first visit

Ruins at Philippi, approximately fifteen miles inland from Neapolis and on the Via Egnatia. Paul arrived here at about A.D. 49 and with the help of Aquila and Priscilla established the first church that we know about in Europe.

of Paul's to Philippi, he writes to them and says, "I thank my God upon every remembrance of you, always in every prayer of mine for you all making request with joy, for your fellowship in the gospel from the first day until now" (Phil. 1:3–5). Friendly hospitality is a powerful form of Christian witness!

Paul and Silas Arrested.

The scene shifts drastically now from Lydia to a demented slave girl. Her apparent ability to tell fortunes was exploited by her masters who profited from her "spirit of divination." When Paul commanded the spirit to come out of her in the name of Jesus Christ and she was healed, her masters were furious and charged Paul and Silas with disturbing the peace and being troublemakers. Since the Roman authorities prided themselves on their ability to maintain order, anyone accused of causing trouble and of being a public nuisance was dealt with severely—Paul and Silas were arrested and beaten. They were then put in chains and thrown into jail. This was their thanks for restoring sanity to a slave girl.

The drama now moves toward its climax. Paul and Silas didn't act like flogged prisoners—they prayed and sang praises unto God. And at midnight, Luke tells us, there was a "great earthquake, so that the foundations of the prison were shaken: and immediately all the doors were opened, and everyone's bands were loosed" (16:25–26).

The Conversion of the Jailer.

The jailer was jolted to consciousness by the earthquake, and when he saw all of the doors open, he assumed his prisoners had escaped. Rather than suffer that disgrace, he drew his sword and was ready to kill himself when Paul called out and assured him the prisoners were still there (16:27–28). First, in verse 25 when Paul and Silas were singing and praying, Luke tells us the other prisoners *heard* them. The Greek word Luke used for "heard" is strong—it means "involved listening." Now the terrified jailer *heard* Paul's words of reassurance and was apparently so awed by what had happened that he asked the crucial question, "Sirs, what must I do to be saved?" Back came the answer that has shaken the world from then until now, "Believe on the Lord Jesus Christ, and thou shalt be saved, and thy house" (16:30–31).

The jailer believed. And we know this not just from

The traditional site of the jail in Philippi where Paul and Barnabas were incarcerated. It was here that the jailer asked the all-important question, "What must I do to be saved?"

what Luke tells us, but from what the jailer did next. He bathed their wounds and fed them. Frequently, it isn't our words that impress people, but our actions. A Christian is not just a talker—but a doer. We don't know anything more about this jailer than what Luke tells us here, but I don't think it is wild speculation to believe that he told and re-told the story of what happened to him that night.

The scene closes with the jailer telling Paul and Silas that the magistrates have released them. But Paul now advised them of the fact that he and Silas are Roman citizens and, as such, should never have been beaten, and he demanded a public apology.

Yes, like the four missionaries to Philippi, we too will run into all kinds of people as we move through life in our adventure of faith. Some are easy to get along with—others are difficult. But our mission as Christians is to bring healing and joy to everyone who crosses our path.

In It Together at Thessalonica. With the change of pronouns in 17:1 it would appear that Luke stayed behind in Philippi while Paul and Silas and Timothy set out along the Egnatian Way for the city of Thessalonica, modern Salonica. Luke dismisses the trip with just a few words, but it was a distance of between eighty-five and one hundred miles. As we watch while Paul and Silas and Luke minister both in Thessalonica and Berea, we will begin to see an undercurrent of relationship between them and the new Christians, which can best be described, I believe, by the Greek word *koinonia*, usually translated "fellowship" (17:1–15).

Upon arrival in Thessalonica Paul spent three weeks teaching in the synagogue to the Jews with virtually no results except from a few gentiles who responded from the sidelines. However, Paul continued his efforts and his hearers were soon divided into two distinct categories—those who accepted his message gladly and those who didn't and wanted to cause trouble. It is in this kind of a setting that we begin to get our first indication of the nature of Christian fellowship. True *koinonia* is based on the fact that *together we have decided to follow Jesus.* Community is usually based on common experience, and under the teaching of the missionaries, the believers in Thessalonica became a church noted for its spirit of fellowship.

Another peculiarity of fellowship seen here is that it holds up under pressure. Remember, these were new Christians, but when the unbelieving opposition set out to make trouble, Jason and his fellow Christians didn't cave in and renege—a true sign of the kind of fellowship that holds firm under severe pressure (17:6–9).

There is nothing like opposition to draw us together in a true spirit of fellowship. A more recent example of this was seen in the civil rights movement of the 1960s. Blacks and whites were drawn together in a common cause. Freedom was the issue, and while in many places the cost was high, people were drawn together in fellowship under pressure. And today we catch hints every once in a while of the spirit of fellowship that binds Christians in the Russian bloc together as they attempt to live out their faith in a hostile and atheistic culture.

In the midst of the pressure and controversy in Thessalonica we find a most descriptive statement as to the effectiveness of the Christian faith. It was said of the missionaries and the new Christians that they "turned the world upside down" (17:6). They saw in this new Christian faith and fellowship a power that could change the world. Christianity was then, and still is, a power that can both change people's lives and the world around them.

From Thessalonica, Paul and his party moved on another forty-five miles west along the Roman road to Berea (17:10). Here we see that they were received more graciously at first, and Paul had the opportunity to open up the Scriptures to them daily and many believed (17:11–12). But so bitter had been the Jewish opposition in Thessalonica that, apparently, when they heard of Paul's success in Berea, they arrived on the scene and stirred up the people to such a frenzy that Paul had to leave. Silas and Timothy did, however, stay behind for a time to minister to the new Christians.

While we do not face the kind of opposition Paul experienced here, I feel a great need for a new spirit of *koinonia* in our Christian fellowship today. Our strength as Christians comes in pulling together. We draw strength and a sense of purpose from each other. This doesn't mean that we will all think alike or worship alike or act alike, but it does mean that in Christ we are one—we experience a true fellowship with believers—sons and daughters of God—wherever they are.

A Reasonable Faith: Paul in Athens.

I can't help but be amazed at Paul's courage. From the time of his conversion until now, he had been virtually driven from six cities because of opposition to his ministry. And yet he pressed on relentlessly. Now he was on his way alone to Athens. It was a long trip, more than 300 miles. In a sense, all of Paul's debates and encounters were mere preludes to this first Athens event. God's redirection of his ministry was taking him to the capital of Greek culture and philosophy. As Paul moves toward Athens and then as he takes his message there in the summer of A.D. 51, there are four things that stand out in my mind.

First of all, *Paul was willing to go to Athens*. When Paul left Berea, Athens wasn't the only place he could have gone. But he *chose* to go there. After all, his call as an apostle hadn't ruled out any country, culture, or mindset. His brand of Christianity was one of initiative and penetration. While Athens was an intellectual center, it was also a hotbed of pagan worship. There were probably more statues of pagan gods in this city than Paul had seen throughout all of his travels. But he knew there were no people anywhere "unfit" for the gospel. And he was aggressive in his efforts to reach new converts even as he was anxious for Christians to get along together in unity. There was nothing elitist or exclusive about Paul's faith.

The Agora, or "Market," where Paul disputed daily with the scholars of Athens. It was adjacent to the Areopagus (Mars Hill) on the north and the Acropolis on the east.

The Acropolis was the architectural heart of Athens. Its primary building was the Parthenon, which was built with Pentelic marble and magnificently decorated with sculptures.

When Paul actually arrived in Athens, we catch something of his feelings as Luke writes, "...his spirit was stirred in him, when he saw the city wholly given to idolatry" (17:16). And we next find him meeting and talking with people in the synagogue and in the marketplace.

Second, *Paul met them on their own turf*. He was equal to the Athenian give-and-take. Paul quickly adjusted to the discourses that dated back to the times of Socrates, and entered into the lively discussions wherever they oc-

It was "in the midst of Mars Hill"—the Areopagus—that Paul delivered his outstanding address to the "men of Athens." Mars Hill, in the foreground, is located on the west side of the Acropolis, which can be seen in the background of this picture.

curred. This soon brought him to the attention of the Epicureans and the Stoics (17:18). Both philosophies dated back to between 200 and around 300 B.C. When their adherents heard that an advocate of a new religion had arrived in town, they were curious. They took him to the

Areopagus (Mars Hill), and it was there that Paul was given the opportunity to explain his faith, "May we know what this new doctrine, whereof thou speakest, is? For thou bringest certain strange things to our ears: we would know therefore what these things mean" (17:19–20). Paul, now meeting them on their own ground, appealed to them in a way that was consistent with their own philosophies. He knew those philosophers were attracted by novelty. So he proclaimed "a new doctrine"—he offered a new and better philosophy.

In speaking, Paul was respectful and courteous. He made reference to their altar to The Unknown God as a means of contact and of getting their attention. He talked their language and quoted from their writings, and then he moved in, tactfully yet boldly declaring the truth of the gospel of Christ. He offered them a better way, and that is the mission of Christianity—it is our mission today.

In practical terms Christianity is relating Christ with His transforming power to *every* part of life. That is why I believe a Charles Colson attempting to relate Christ to prison situations is a model of what each of us are to do from the vantage point of our own vocation. Other models for us include Senator Mark Hatfield who relates Christianity to politics . . . a Mother Teresa who ministers to the suffering of her world . . . a Joni Eareckson who speaks especially to the physically handicapped. And then, of course, there was Paul, the philosopher, who was so effective when ministering to the intellectuals in Athens. Our vocation or work, whatever it is, gives us a base for effective witnessing.

Third, *Paul approached his listeners with general affirmation*. Paul's opening remarks on Mars Hill illustrate his affirmative ability to make contact with his listeners (17:22). The wording here is dated, for what Paul really said was, "I can tell that you are very religious." This was obvious, for there were altars and statues of gods and goddesses throughout all of Athens, and the Parthenon, that great temple of Athena, dominated the city and the surrounding countryside from its place of prominence on the Acropolis—just above Mars Hill. In their way they were reaching out to make contact with the divine. Paul very wisely recognized this and used it as a bridge to proclaim the truth of the one God, the Creator of the universe.

Paul's example here is a good one for us. Too often in our

witness to people we either say or give the impression that "You've really messed things up" or "I can tell that you've really missed it." To condemn or act superior as if we have all the truth alienates people. It cuts them off and cuts them out and our contact is lost. Paul was too wise for this. He had earned the right to their attention.

Fourth, *Paul used the bridge to carry the greater message.* Having made contact with his listeners, Paul now shares his faith (17:24–31). From his reference to creation (17:24), which was a common ground of agreement among those philosophers, he moved them along to the truth in Jesus Christ. Following the conclusion of Paul's sermon, Luke shares with us the reaction of the crowd, "And when they heard of the resurrection of the dead, some mocked: and others said, We will hear thee again of this matter (17:32). As would be expected, there are always those who reject outright the message of Christ, but as on Mars Hill, there are also those who readily accept it or remain open.

In our study of the Gospels we saw again and again how sensitive Jesus was to His listeners—He talked their language and they understood Him. So far in our study of Acts we have observed, as well, Paul's sensitivity to his hearers—his approach was always tailored to them. But his message of salvation through Christ was the same.

Obstacles and Opportunities:
Paul in Corinth.

Paul is on the move again as he leaves Athens and travels to Corinth. This great metropolis was one of the major cities in the Roman empire at that time. It was strategically located on a narrow isthmus that separated northern and southern Greece. Corinth was a majestic city dominated by the towering Acrocorinthus, a rocky hill on which was built a fortress and Aphrodite's temple.

In this final part of our lesson now, which includes this first visit of Paul to Corinth, we will have the opportunity to see how God can turn obstacles into opportunities. We will also see how we can and should respond when the unexpected happens in our lives. Admittedly, our perspectives are limited. But certain events in our lesson now remind us that when a given situation or set of circumstances appear to be a hindrance or setback, it may become an opportunity that God can use for our growth.

When Paul arrived in Corinth, he was fortunate enough to make contact with Aquila and Priscilla, a Jewish couple

Ruins of the ancient city of Corinth, located on a narrow isthmus between the Saronic Gulf on the east and the Corinthian Gulf on the west. In the background is the 2,000 foot high Acrocorinthus, on which the temple of Aphrodite stood.

who had been forced to leave Italy when Claudius had banished the Jews in A.D. 49 (18:2). Relocating their home must have been a traumatic experience for this couple, but they were now well settled in as tentmakers. And since this was Paul's vocation, their common skills brought them together. At any rate, the persecution that forced Aquila and Priscilla to leave Italy became God's opportunity for them to meet Paul.

Paul soon settled in with Aquila and Priscilla and Luke tells us he preached and taught in the synagogue, witnessing to the truth that Jesus was the Messiah (18:4). After a time he experienced a glad reunion with Silas and Timothy. But evidently, not long after their arrival, Jewish opposition to their message became so strong and bitter that Paul said, "Your blood be upon your own heads; I am clean: from henceforth I will go unto the Gentiles" (18:6). Once again for Paul, the obstacle of opposition became an opportunity.

Luke tells us that Paul began to minister next door to the synagogue (18:7), and it wasn't long before Crispus, the ruler of the synagogue, became a believer in Jesus. Be-

Ruins in the city of Corinth which Paul first visited in A.D. 51. This was a busy city in those days, and it served as headquarters for the Roman proconsul.

*An intricately carved piece of marble among the ruins in Corinth. It
is possible this was originally a part of an upright column.*

cause of this conversion, other Jews in Corinth accepted
Christ, and Paul received a great affirmation from the Lord
(18:9–10) that we can take for ourselves today. And it was
this affirmation that inspired Paul to remain in Corinth for
a year and a half.

I've been thinking a great deal about the seeming insignificant events in our lives, which from God's perspective
may not be insignificant at all. Take, for example, the cold
and damp evening when a faithful layman conducted
what might have been considered a rather insignificant
church service. But after reading the text and explaining it,
a ragged neighborhood boy responded to the invitation to
accept Christ as his Saviour. There was no other response,

but that boy was Charles Spurgeon who became the great preacher and evangelist. A chain of events started that night that continues even now.

Then there was the downhearted Sunday school teacher in Chicago who thought he wasn't getting anywhere with his class. But one boy, Dwight L. Moody, responded to his message, and with that, another chain of events was started that still goes on. These and other similar events remind us that when circumstances force change on us, when big opportunities seem to disappear, God may be opening a new door. Remember, it was Paul's setback in the synagogue that led him to an even greater ministry in Corinth.

Luke gives us one more scene in Corinth before Paul starts his trip home. Gallio, the Roman proconsul, enters the scene. It is likely he had just arrived in Corinth after having received his appointment in A.D. 51. Luke tells us that the Jews who opposed Paul and his teaching took this opportunity to try to get a judgment against Paul. But here we find an excellent example of Roman justice. Gallio saw through the duplicity of the Jews and doubtless had inquired into Paul's character, for Gallio threw the case out of court and ruled in Paul's favor (18:12–17).

The Journey's End (18:18–22)

From Corinth to Caesarea.

Finally, the time came for Paul to leave. He took a ship and, accompanied by Aquila and Priscilla, traveled across the Aegean Sea to Ephesus. The stop there was brief, but there was still time for Paul to speak in the synagogue. Evidently, Aquila and Priscilla remained in Ephesus. But Paul continued on by ship to Caesarea and then traveled overland to Antioch in Syria.

Paul's second missionary journey had taken the best part of three years. He had traveled a little over 3,000 miles—about 1,200 on the sea and almost 1,800 on land. And, undoubtedly, the land travel was all on foot. It had been a long and hard trip, but the gospel of Christ now had taken root in Europe under the guidance of the Holy Spirit.

It has been well said that when we look into the future, our vision is blurred, but hindsight is always 20/20. This lesson has illustrated that truth for us. As with Paul and the early disciples, there is an unseen Presence Who guides our steps. There is an unfelt Hand that supports us along the way and a quiet and sometimes unnoticed Voice that says, "This is the way, walk in it." And we find inspiration in this lesson to believe that as we are obedient to God and follow His leading, He will use us in unexpected ways in the magnificent drama of life.

Give me that Spirit that sings in even the worst of circumstances. Fill me with more of Yourself. AMEN.

WHAT THIS SCRIPTURE MEANS TO ME—
Acts 15:36—18:22

"Permission to descend to 10,000 feet," the pilot of the small private plane radioed, "on approach for landing."

"Roger, message confirmed," the speaker crackled. "Turn right, heading one-seven-zero. Alternate destination request approved. Do you have a problem?"

The pilot paused for a moment. What would the control tower say when he told them there was nothing wrong, that he just had a feeling he ought to get down as fast as he could? He glanced at the businessmen behind him. How would he explain this delay to them?

The pilot reached for his radio. "I think I have a faulty gauge here, and I'm unsure of my fuel level." This wasn't true, but in the strangeness of the moment he didn't know what other excuse to offer.

"Roger," the tower replied. "Clearance to land on runway two-niner."

The landing was routine. He pulled up to the hangar, frantically searching for an explanation of any kind while berating himself for listening to "a feeling." Suddenly, he heard a gasp behind him. One of the men, ashen in color and with his hand on his heart, slumped in his seat.

The man was rushed to a nearby hospital. And only later did the pilot learn that the short time between the heart attack and treatment made the difference between life and death. If they had still been in the air when the man was attacked, he would probably have died. A powerful feeling—a "still small voice"—had made the difference.

Twice in this Scripture lesson Luke reports that the Spirit stopped Paul from going into certain places to preach. Then, we see as well that when the Spirit gave positive direction, Paul was quick to follow. It was like that when he went to Macedonia. The guidance was clear, and even though he was thrown into prison, and run out of town, he met with huge success.

The Spirit—the still, small voice—often doesn't come as forcefully to us as it did that day to Paul. I remember how I struggled a few years back trying to decide whether or not I should quit a secure job that I really enjoyed to go back to school. Everyone I knew was pressed for their opinion. I wore out logic trying to figure out the "best" solution. But in the end, I listened to Something deep within me—Something I couldn't ignore, no matter how hard I tried.

In response, I quit the job and moved 800 miles away to a strange place and a small apartment. The very first night of school I got into an argument with another student over the merits of the job I'd just left. In my loneliness and confusion I couldn't help but wonder if I'd made the right choice.

But just a year later, I'd married the young lady with whom I argued that first night and had gone back to my old job. Now, though, my life was richer than I could have ever imagined—all because of Something inside me I couldn't ignore.

So often, even though we know better, we forget and get all worked up when looking for an answer to a difficult problem. We may search frantically through the Bible for guidance, read books, and get opinions from friends. But, for me, at least, it isn't until I get quiet and listen to God in the silence that I can begin to find my answer—and His will for me. Unlike the pilot in our story we have no need to rationalize or stretch the truth when we follow the inner voice which comes from God.

LESSON 6
ACTS 18:23—20:38

Strengthening the Fellowship: Paul's Third Missionary Journey

Master, Thank You for Your joy, which is my strength. AMEN.

There is a great deal of emphasis today on the need to be well-informed. In fact, millions of people are involved in some form of what we call continuing education.

It is not uncommon for people in mid-life to return to school to further their education. Many women when faced with the empty nest return to the classroom. Short term motivational and training seminars are increasingly popular. And thousands, if not millions, are enrolled in courses offered on television by reputable institutions of learning.

Behind all of this, I believe, is the recognition that we cannot stand still. Either we grow or we fall prey to inertia and slip into decline. The Apostle Paul was apparently well aware that growth was essential in the spiritual life of the new Christians in the churches he had founded and nurtured.

Our last lesson closed with Paul's return to Syrian Antioch after his second missionary journey. Now Luke writes, "And after he had spent some time there, he departed, and went over all the country of Galatia and Phrygia in order, strengthening all the disciples" (18:23). Once again Paul is on the move as he strikes out from Antioch, heading for his home city of Tarsus. From there he makes his way over the Taurus mountains, through the narrow and arduous Cilician Gates, and into southern Galatia. Moving west steadily, he evidently visited with and instructed groups of believers wherever he could find them.

Luke doesn't give us any detail on these visits except to indicate that Paul kept moving west into Phrygia where he continued his nurturing and teaching ministry. Paul knew that a failure to follow up would result in a loss of power and vitality among these Asia Minor Christians and churches. During this time he was not only preaching salvation, but was actively engaged in his own style of "continuing education."

Completing the Picture (18:23–19:10)

Luke breaks away from his narrative now and introduces a new character. By doing so he draws attention to the gaps that existed in the lives of some believers in spite of the apostle's progress. This next part of our lesson gives us two examples of how Paul labored to bring new Chris-

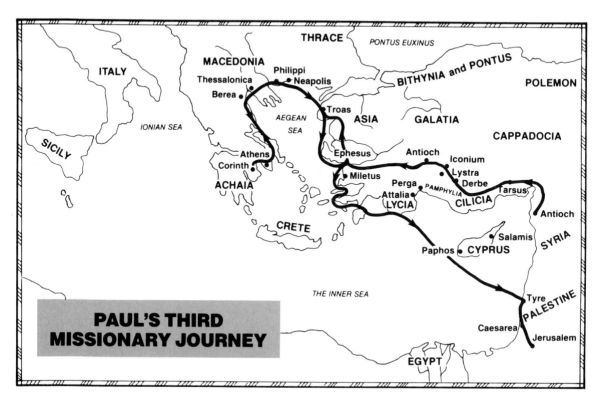

PAUL'S THIRD MISSIONARY JOURNEY

tians into a more complete understanding and experience of the faith.

The first example centers on the person of Apollos. In just a few words Luke gives us an amazing portrait of this Jew from Alexandria, a city founded by Alexander the Great in 332 B.C. With the passing years this Egyptian city had become a haven for expatriated Jews. Its population in the first century was about 1,000,000, of which some 400,000 were Jews.

Introducing Apollos.

Alexandria was a great university center that offered rich resources of learning. In fact it was Alexandrian scholars who gave the world the Septuagint, the oldest Greek version of the Old Testament. This was the atmosphere in which Apollos obtained his education.

In his brief biographical sketch Luke tells us that Apollos was eloquent, was highly trained in the Scriptures, was religiously learned, was fervent in spirit, and was a good teacher (18:24–25). From that glowing description we can see that he was a paragon of religious virtue.

We meet Apollos in the ancient city of Ephesus where he was teaching and preaching in the synagogue, but Luke gives us a clue that something is missing when he says that Apollos knew "only the baptism of John" (18:25). This tells us that Apollos was a disciple of John the Baptist, and as such he followed carefully the strict rules for life and conduct that were observed by the members of the Baptist's sect. Apollos understood baptism for repentance, and he knew *about* Jesus. And what he knew, Apollos represented well and with eloquent enthusiasm, but when Aquila and Priscilla heard him, they saw that something was missing. And they knew what it was.

Like John the Baptist, Apollos called people to leave behind their former ways of thinking and living. They were to repent—turn around and head in a new direction, but the message stopped there. It told them what they should leave behind; it did not tell them what they should embrace.

Aquila and Priscilla saw that while Apollos understood about baptism for repentance, he did not know about, and he hadn't experienced, the baptism of the Holy Spirit. And while he was apparently being used by the Lord to lead people to repentance, his ministry was incomplete and lacked power. And so Luke tells us that the very wise and spir-

What is left today of a marble paved main street in Ephesus. At the time of Paul this street was lined with magnificent buildings and ran from the harbor to the great amphitheater.

itually mature Aquila and Priscilla took him aside "and expounded unto him the way of God more perfectly" (18:26).

Now we see something in this remarkable man that commends him even further. Not only was he a good teacher, but it would appear that he was also *teachable*. There is no hint in Luke's brief mention that he resisted the instruction of Aquila and Priscilla. After all, with all of his talent it would have been easy for him to feel offended. With the success he had experienced so far, it would have been quite understandable for him to protest, "What do I need to be instructed about?" But instead, he quietly submitted to the guidance of these new spiritual mentors of his and entered into a whole new experience of faith. And while Luke doesn't describe what happened, he writes about the results as Apollos left Ephesus and ministered throughout southern Greece: "...the brethren wrote, exhorting the disciples to receive him: who, when he was come, *helped them much which had believed through grace: for he mightily convinced the Jews, and that publickly, showing by the scriptures that Jesus was Christ:* (18:27–28, italics mine).

Now, Apollos had the power to help the new Christians, and he had come, through the guidance of the Holy Spirit, to a new belief that Jesus was indeed the Christ—the Messiah.

We've spent quite a bit of time in this part of our lesson on the Apollos story, but I think for good reason. From the brief biographical sketch Luke gave us of Apollos, we saw that he was well educated, had a good knowledge of the Scriptures, and was a gifted leader and communicator. But that was not enough for him, and it isn't for us. We may know a lot *about* Jesus but not really *know* Him in the power of the Holy Spirit. With us, as with Apollos, the power to live a rich, fulfilled, and productive Christian life comes only through the presence of the indwelling Jesus Who has become Lord as well as Saviour.

Paul Begins His Ministry in Ephesus.

Now we pick up again on the Apostle Paul. We left him earlier moving west through Galatia and Phrygia in Asia Minor (modern Turkey). Luke brings us together now as Paul arrives in Ephesus. You remember that he had stopped off briefly here on his way home from the second missionary journey. Undoubtedly, what Paul saw on his first brief visit convinced him that he wanted to return soon and spend more time there.

In Paul's day Ephesus was already at least 1,000 years old. It was a magnificent city, and in Roman times was the capital of the province of Asia. Its architecture was superb, but its most majestic building was the Temple of Artemis (Diana), which was one of the Seven Wonders of the World. Even by today's standards it was a large building—220 feet wide by 425 feet long, and it stood more than fifty feet high. The city was a center for idol worship, and the cult of Artemis was morally degrading, with its prostitute-priestesses and pagan practices.

Even today a visitor to Ephesus is awed by the ruins that remain and by what is left of the marble pavement that once formed the streets of that bustling, ancient city.

It was to this throbbing and thriving city that Paul now came. And it was here that he spent three important years of his life. But let's pick up on the drama now as Luke has given it to us.

Upon Paul's arrival in Ephesus he makes contact with certain of the Ephesian Christians, and this brings us to the second illustration in our lesson of incompleteness. Evidently, it was apparent to Paul that something was missing in their lives, and so he asked, "Have ye received the Holy Ghost since ye believed?" (19:2). They immediately responded that they didn't know anything about the Holy Ghost—all they were aware of was the baptism of John the Baptist. They had obeyed and believed as far as they knew to go. But as Paul explained, that wasn't enough, so now he opened up to them the Good News of the gospel of Jesus Christ. They were anxious to complete their faith and they believed and were baptized again "in the name of the Lord Jesus" (19:5). And it was then that the Holy Spirit came upon them with great power (19:6).

From the insights given us here in this part of our lesson we see the importance of being complete in our faith and of helping others to know that same experience. We have learned that in Christ we are saved *from* something—sin, and we are also saved *for* something—righteousness. We are moving from being saved by faith to living by faith. Our viewpoint is shifting from looking backward to the beginning point to looking forward to the full challenges of being a Christian indwelt by the living Lord. And it is then that we move from membership to discipleship—a quality of life and a depth of commitment that comes from experiencing wholeness through Christ in the Christian way of life.

Now these twelve men had moved from a process (the baptism of John) to a Person (the Holy Spirit). They had moved from ritual to power and beyond *an* experience to the *ongoing vitality* of *the* experience. And this was made possible for them, and for us, by a continuing relationship with Christ, and that is made possible by the Holy Spirit.

There is a renewal, I believe, in the Church today of an emphasis on completeness in the Spirit. More and more

The ruins of Hadrian's Temple in Ephesus located along the main, marble paved street.

we hear such terms as Christian maturity, growth in Christ-likeness, spiritual formation, and so on. There is a yeasty movement within the Body of Christ for which we can be thankful even though our world is turbulent.

Following his experience with the twelve men who had been followers of John the Baptist, Paul immediately turned his attention to a concentrated teaching and preaching schedule in the synagogue in Ephesus. Few details are given us about this period except Luke writes that after three months a dispute arose among the Jews over his teaching and Paul had to discontinue his synagogue ministry. But he then moved his headquarters to the school of Tyrannus, a philosopher of considerable note.

Paul's Ministry in Ephesus (19:11–20:1)

Confronting the Counterfeit Spirit.

The Christian life is not limited only by the incomplete interpretations of it but also by certain counterfeits, which are either a part of it or are in competition with it. In this next part of our lesson we will look at some of these counterfeits. And we will see from this that frequently within the fellowship of Christians we will come up against spiritual frauds.

The first incident might be entitled, "Confronting the Counterfeit Spirit" (19:13–20).

Ephesus was a center of superstition and sorcery. And with all of the mighty works that Paul did there in the name of Jesus, it was only natural that these works would attract the attention of some of the corrupt rascals who were involved in magic-for-profit schemes. Apparently, Sceva and his sons—all renegade Jews—had seen some of Paul's miracles, and they attempted to duplicate them by invoking Jesus' name even though they didn't believe in Him (19:13). The results of this skulduggery were disastrous even though there is a hint of humor in what happened. When the rascals commanded an evil spirit to come out of a person, "the evil spirit answered and said, Jesus I know, and Paul I know; but who are ye?" (19:15). And with that the possessed man attacked Sceva and his sons with such furor that they were hurt and had to run for their lives (19:16).

The exposure of these counterfeits, which so vividly illustrated the difference between sorcery and magic and the miracles performed in Jesus' name, impressed everyone in the city. And Luke tells us that many of them became believers and burned their books of magic and their charms.

What does this rather strange (from our point of view) story have to say to us today? I think it has a practical application because in a way the problem behind this incident is still with us. Unfortunately, we don't have to look too far before we see someone attempting to exercise the power of the gospel without having had the experience. And there are those who use the language without having participated in the realities of the Christian life. And, of course, there are those who profess a faith in God but who never act it out in daily living.

Then, too, there are people who have seen the disastrous results of trying to call on a power they do not possess. And like their Ephesian predecessors (19:19), they are now trading in their superstition and magic for the real thing—they are exchanging "churchianity" for authentic Christianity. And now, as then, when this exchange takes place, the Word of God grows mightily and prevails (19:20), both in individual lives and in the total witness of the church.

As we turn back to the Scripture lesson now, Luke seems to insert a two verse parenthesis (19:21–22) in his description of these Ephesian events. Although Paul has a passionate concern for the people to Ephesus, his mind wanders to Greece and Jerusalem—and even to Rome. He has long wanted to personally visit the Imperial City. For years he has traveled the Roman roads in Asia Minor and Greece—now he longed to see the terminus of those roads and preach the gospel there! But it isn't the Lord's time for Paul to leave, so he sends two representatives to Greece, but he remains in Ephesus.

We come now to the second confrontation in this part of our lesson (19:24–41). This can be titled "Confronting the Counterfeit Spirits." The wrong use of the name of Jesus was not the only problem confronting the church in Ephesus. There was a counterfeiting of religion through the production of "spirits" (idols) designed by Ephesian craftsmen. But as a result of Paul's preaching, the demand for the silver shrines of Diana was diminishing and so was the profit for those who made and sold them. And all of this created a crisis between the counterfeit deities of Ephesian culture and their makers, and the Christians who were faithful to their Lord.

Luke now introduces a new character, Demetrius, who was not only a spokesman for the "Silversmith Association" but was a spellbinder of an orator (19:25–27). He knew that if Christianity flourished, he and his fellow craftsmen would go broke. He had heard the word that wherever Paul went he insisted that there are "no gods, which are made with hands." This was a crisis that had to be met, so Demetrius whipped up the crowd until a full-fledged riot was in the making.

After all, to have their profit-making business disrupted was a serious matter that had to be handled quickly. But

Confronting the Counterfeit Spirits-Idols.

111

there was another issue here that was equally touchy. With clever rhetoric Demetrius pointed out that if the Christians got the upper hand, their image as a city would be downgraded in all of Asia (19:27). There was an "Ephesian Way" that had to be preserved. Jesus challenged that way by undercutting the very foundations of paganism in Ephesus and all of Asia.

The Showdown at the Amphitheater.

Luke gives us a graphic description of the scene provoked by Demetrius' rhetoric. The crowd became angry and began to chant, "Great is Diana of the Ephesians." This apparently ignited the emotional furor of the crowd, and they seized Paul's two Greek companions and rushed to the great theater (19:29).It is not unlikely that it was

The great amphitheater in Ephesus that seated 25,000. It was here that the mob gathered to protest the preaching of the gospel that was ruining the sale of their idols.

jammed to its capacity of 25,000. Luke indicates that Paul was not in the crowd at the time all of this was going on, but evidently when he heard what was happening, he wanted to go and speak to them. But both his fellow Christians and "certain of the chief of Asia"—the Asiarchs, which were elected officials for the province—persuaded Paul not to put in an appearance (19:30–31).

The crowd that filled the theater was evidently confused as to what to do next. In fact, Luke tells us that many of them didn't even know why they were there—they had just seen a crowd and heard the noise and followed. Finally, they picked up again on the chant, "Great is Diana of the Ephesians." There's something hypnotic about a crowd that moves and chants in unison, and apparently the "town clerk" was afraid things would get completely out of control. And as we've already seen, this was something Rome would not put up with, so he pleaded with the crowd to calm down and not resort to violence but let the normal process of Roman law take its course—Demetrius and his fellow craftsmen could file charges and the tribunal would make its ruling (19:35–41). The voice of authority broke through their confused state, and the crowd broke up.

On the surface the meaning for us from this whole event might seem a bit obscure, but there are certain important lessons here for us—there's much about the "Ephesian Syndrome" that exists in our world today. There is a tendency to keep Jesus in the background if He and His teachings interfere with our comfort and with our profit. It has been said that the hardest thing to convert is our pocketbook. If a threat of any kind to our materialistic god comes on the scene, we tend to revolt and rationalize our way out.

And, like the Ephesians, we don't want our image and our way disturbed. We build our national, cultural, and denominational fences so high that not only do we shut others out, but we can't see out ourselves. But this was not the vision Jesus passed along to His disciples, and it was not Paul's vision. The Christian vision is to the whole world. It doesn't shut people out, and it doesn't exploit them. At the same time we must stand firmly, as did the Ephesian Christians, against the counterfeit "spirits," the idols, the alternative gods, that threaten our Christian walk. And above all, we late twentieth-century Christians must carefully guard against attempting to reshape Jesus to fit our situation.

Paul's long stay at Ephesus had now wound down to a close. It had been a time of victory but also a time of stress. In just a few words now, though, Luke gives us a glimpse of a tender scene (20:1). Before leaving Ephesus and closing out his three-year ministry, "Paul called unto him the disciples, and *embraced them*" (italics mine). These Christian friends had come to mean a great deal to him and they had been through a lot together as they took their stand against the paganism in Ephesus. The love and support of Christian friends is one of our richest treasures.

Confirming the Saints (20:2–20:38)

Exhortation and Encouragement in Greece.

We pick up momentum now as Paul moves out on the final leg of this third missionary journey. We're told that his route took him to Macedonia where he undoubtedly ministered to the churches in Philippi, Thessalonica, and Berea. And from there he evidently traveled south to Achaia, probably spending most of his time in Corinth.

Throughout Paul's brief visit with the Christians in Greece his ministry had been one of exhortation (20:2) and encouragement. But he was headed toward Jerusalem now. However, just as he was about to take a boat bound for Syria, a plot against his life was exposed, and instead he headed back north from Corinth, overland, to Macedonia where he and a deputation from the churches there sailed from Neapolis to Troas (20:3–4). And here he continues the ministry of encouragement and confirmation that had marked his visit in Greece. At this stage of its development, encouragement and confirmation were vital for the future of the Christian community in the Graeco-Roman world. Let's watch now the method Paul uses in extending this part of his ministry as he moves toward Jerusalem.

The Eutychus Miracle in Troas.

First, we see *confirmation through power* in the incident involving Eutychus (20:7–12). The Christians at Troas came together for worship and to hear Paul. The communion service and the sermon were long. In an effort to stay awake young Eutychus positioned himself in an open window in "the third loft" where he hoped the breeze off the Aegean would keep him awake. But after a time he dozed off and fell to the floor below and was pronounced dead. But Luke then assures us that Paul took charge of things: "And Paul went down, and embracing him said, Trouble not yourselves; for his life is in him" (20:10). What at first seemed to be an unnecessary tragedy was turned into another opportunity to glorify God and confirm the power of the gospel as Eutychus' life was restored to him.

Confirmation through power is still a necessary ingredient in the strengthening of Christians. I have a young friend who in a moment of discouragement asked, "Why don't we see miracles happening today like they did in the time of Paul?" On the surface this seems like a hard question to answer. But when we stop to really think about it on a deep level, we are reminded that God is at work in a miraculous way even in our world today. People are being touched by the power of the gospel and are being healed physically, emotionally, and spiritually. And this is happening wherever cold and formalized religion is replaced by the warm spirit of the early Church, where a long sermon and a healing miracle were compatible with the faith.

This is not to say that we should try to manufacture miracles. Our faith should not be based on whether or not miracles, by our definition, occur. Jesus warned against that. Rather, our faith should have its roots in the kind of a dynamism that says to people, "There's something powerful, transforming, and life-changing about Christianity." May it be said of us as it was of the disciples in Thessalonica, "These that have turned the world upside down."

Next, we see that Paul brought about *confirmation through proclamation*. Paul is on the move again as he travels from Troas to Miletus. Here he wants a last visit with the elders of the Ephesian church so he sends word and asks them to join him (20:17–35). In this farewell proclamation Paul stresses the importance of spiritual growth. For me, the key verse in the speech is verse 32: "And now, brethren, I commend you to God, and to the word of his grace, which is able to build you up, and to give you an inheritance among all them which are sanctified."

But let's look more closely now at this part of our lesson, for in it we see certain important ingredients of confirmation. Paul begins by referring to the credibility and integrity of his own life (20:18–20). He reminds the Ephesian elders of his faithfulness to God. In doing this he wasn't giving vent to egotism or self-centeredness. Rather, he

The Stopover at Miletus.

was stating the simple fact that words and actions must go together. There can be no greater encouragement than to see God at work in the life of a fellow Christian. And in verse 21 he tells them, and us, that it is "repentance toward God, and faith toward our Lord Jesus Christ," which makes that quality of life possible. In other words, exemplary living is made possible through extravagant grace.

Next, Paul reminds his Ephesian friends that adversity awaits him and all who follow in the way of Christ (20:23–29). Paul was moving confidently toward Jerusalem although he knew that trouble and affliction was ahead. Verse 24 is a powerful testimony of the work of God in Paul's life, "But none of these things move me, neither count I my life dear unto myself, so that I might finish my course with joy, and the ministry, which I have received of the Lord Jesus, to testify the gospel of the grace of God." What a marvelous benediction as he tells these friends that he probably will never see them again. But his words were more than a benediction—he knew they would face hard times, even as we do. The Bible gives us no assurance that the payoff for the Christian is a trouble-free life, but we do have the assurance that God's grace is equal to every part of life.

I believe this witness of Paul's is important for us today. There is sort of a "prosperity theology" going around that seems to encourage Christians to believe the illusion that God verifies the reality of faith by guaranteeing wealth, health, and other forms of material gain. And the reverse side of that coin says that if we are not enjoying these "blessings," it is a sign of insufficient faith. But this goes against everything that Paul has taught us and what he says here.

Paul moves next to urge the Ephesian elders toward a high quality of leadership (20:28–32). The words, "take heed" and "feed the church" in verse 28 are significant. In "taking heed" they and we are called to a life of watchfulness—we are to be sensitive to the subtleties of temptation. And the words, "feed the church" speak of the need to nurture people—each other—in the Lord. We are to build each other up and encourage each other. This attitude is the direct opposite of so much that we see. There is no room for infighting in an atmosphere of encouragement and love.

Paul isn't home yet from this third missionary journey —that comes in the next lesson—but throughout this trip he has given us a powerful example of what it means to live and witness for Christ. Now in verse 36 we have the third aspect of Paul's ministry, the *confirmation of prayer*. He is telling us that prayer is the lifeline of faith and strength. Prayer has sustained his life, it has empowered him for service, and it has strengthened him in times of suffering.

From Paul we learn that words are important, actions are important, but without prayer, nothing is important. It is helpful to remember this in our action-oriented society today. I've seen so many people "work hard for Jesus." I've been through times when I felt I was working *for* Him rather than *with* Him—I've been more of a servant than a son. And I've been frustrated under the "employee syndrome."

Paul knew that the best antidote to Christian burnout was prayer. Without prayer, we soon discover that we're just going through the motions—we respond and act out of habit. Like Samson in the Old Testament, the power has departed from us and we don't even know it (Judg. 16:20).

By Paul's words and actions in this closing scene, his Ephesian friends knew that prayer was the final and ultimate means of confirmation.

For us, the real purpose of prayer is not to get *things* but to get *strength*.

Thank You for using this lesson to strengthen me, Lord. Your powerful Word disciples and nurtures me. AMEN.

WHAT THIS SCRIPTURE MEANS TO ME—
Acts 18:23–20:38

Her resume would hardly set her apart from others. It would simply identify Louise Degrafinried as a wife, a mother, and a farmer with a small cotton patch in a rural county in Tennessee. You would have little reason to recognize her name. But after meeting Louise, I shall never forget it.

I had gone to visit Louise at her home to hear the story of how she had convinced an escaped convict, who had broken into her home with a gun, to surrender to the police without a struggle. "I just gave him Jesus," Louise told me.

When I drove away from Louise and Nathan Degrafinried's home that night, I wasn't thinking about what a great story I'd just heard. Instead, I was impressed with Louise as a person. I had come to see that Louise had such a deep faith in God that it had become a part of her very existence. For her, faith seemed as natural, and as essential, as taking a breath. And even though it was obvious that life had been hard for Louise, she radiated a genuine and contagious joy.

As I whizzed down the interstate highway, I couldn't help but compare Louise to myself (though I was certain she wouldn't have approved of that at all). When I was a kid, I thought that the true test of a Christian came on Super Bowl Sunday. Often, the game would still be going on when the time came for evening services. A good Christian, I'd decided, would turn off the set and go to church.

Then when I was older I figured that the amount of money one put in the church collection plate was about the truest measuring stick. The more you gave, the better a Christian you were. But as the mile markers on I-40 passed by, I began to see that true faith and commitment—like what Louise had—can't be measured. It can only be lived.

Somehow, I think Paul had learned that lesson too. And it was this section of Acts that helped me realize this. Why? Because among some of the most brutal challenges of Christianity he faced, he didn't counter with measuring sticks. He didn't tell the people what to do; he told them how to live.

Ernest Hollings is a United States senator from South Carolina. For years and years, Hollings says, he read about the problem of hunger in this country and what he could do about it. But he never understood how real it was until he went to a poor area of Charleston, South Carolina. There, he said, he met the hungry. And he discovered he needed to live the problem before he could do anything about it.

Have you read about the woman in a church choir in Des Moines, Iowa who sings louder than anyone else so she can drown out the growls of a stomach that has not had food in two days? What about the man in Newark, New Jersey who brings a bag of clothing to a relief center, even though that leaves him literally with just the shirt on his back? These people remind me of Paul's farewell to the Ephesian elders. "You yourselves know how I lived among you all the time from the first day that I set foot in Asia" (20:18, RSV).

It is here that I find my own challenge as a Christian: to *live* the life that Chirst has put before me, rather than simply *doing* all the right things. I see that I need to be like the publican of Christ's parable, whose faith-filled life said volumes more than the Pharisee's deed-filled prayer.

This lesson of Acts presents us with a tough challenge, but it also explains how to meet it. "And now, brethren, I commend you to God," Paul concluded to those Ephesian elders, "and to the word of his grace, which is able to build you up..." (Acts 20:32).

The challenge. And the means to meet it. Somehow, I think Louise knew it all along. That's just the way she lives!

LESSON 7
ACTS 21:1—26:32

Facing the Enemies

Almighty God, It is difficult to face my enemies. Teach me how to rely on Your strength that I might be able to. AMEN.

On a recent plane trip from Florida to Georgia, I sat next to a man who was one of the fifty-two hostages that had been held for 454 days in Iran. As we conversed, he told me that during his ordeal the real "enemies" were not the captors who confined him, but the thoughts that raced through his own mind. He went on to say that if it had not been for his faith in God and his ability to control his mind (rather than letting it control him), he would never have survived the ordeal.

The Christian faith does not sidestep the fact that sooner or later we must come face-to-face with enemies. This experience has been described variously as "going into the wilderness," "subjected to temptation," or "the dark night of the soul." Sometimes the enemies have been quite tangible, expressing themselves through intense personal misunderstanding and outright persecution. At other times they go under the names of "burnout," "depression," "disease," and "despair." But whatever their name or form, there will inevitably come the time when we as Christians must face enemies of one kind or another.

This fact has been made very clear in our lessons so far

in the book of Acts. But now, as the pace increases, Luke seems to focus in this lesson on the reality of opposition to Christianity as we see the Apostle Paul facing his enemies. Now Paul's opposition moves to center stage, and as we trace his experiences and how he handled them, we will see how, in turn, we are to respond to those who oppose us as we attempt to be faithful to the Lord. In using Acts as something of a manual for maturity and discipleship, we can be thankful to God that the Holy Spirit inspired Luke to deal with this aspect of faith in considerable detail.

Misguided Spirituality (21:1–16)

At the close of our last lesson we left Paul in Miletus on the Asian coast of the Aegean Sea as he was telling his Ephesian friends good-bye. It was a moving scene because Paul had said this was probably the last time they would see each other.

From Miletus to Tyre.

Now, as we pick up on his travels, Luke tells us that Paul's ship sailed south to Coos (Cos), then southwest around the northern tip of the island of Rhodes, and to the port city of Patara in Lycia (21:1). And from there he caught another ship that took him on a straight course around the southeastern tip of Cyprus and on to Tyre on the Phoenician coast (21:2–3). The third missionary journey of Paul was now drawing toward a rapid close, for he was only approximately 120 miles from his final destination—Jerusalem.

Paul Urged Not to Go to Jerusalem.

It was during the week he spent in Tyre that Paul was confronted by "enemies," but this time they were fellow Christians right out of the household of faith (21:4–6). This was a subtle kind of "enemy" and illustrated the *problem of interpretation*. When Paul met with the Christians at Tyre, they "said to Paul through the Spirit, that he should not go up to Jerusalem" (21:4). That is about as clear as it can be, and it appears to have the stamp of the Holy Spirit upon it. If we accept that as it appears on the surface, it would seem that Paul is in error in his determination to travel to Jerusalem. But that isn't the whole picture, and this is why it is so important in our study to make sure everything is taken in context.

On two previous occasions Paul had been instructed and motivated by the Spirit to go to Jerusalem. First, in

Acts 19:21, and then in Acts 20:22 Paul says, "...I go bound in the spirit unto Jerusalem." Now, you will notice in checking both of these verses in the King James text that it says "spirit" rather than "Spirit." This could seem to imply that his decision to go to Jerusalem was based on human desire or determination (his "spirit") rather than by holy direction (God's Spirit). But this is not the case, and the puzzle is cleared up in later translations where the word in those verses is translated "Spirit" or "Holy Spirit."

I don't emphasize this point to quibble, but there is in this story a truth that is important. Paul had been definitely guided by the Holy Spirit to go to Jerusalem. Now, the Christians in Tyre told Paul they had word through the Spirit that he should *not* go to Jerusalem. There seems to be a conflict.

Luke doesn't imply in this story that these sincere Christians hadn't gotten a word from the Lord. They weren't deliberately being deceitful, nor had they failed to hear *something* from the Spirit. But I believe that what happened was that they failed to rightly *interpret* what they heard.

The fact that this can happen shouldn't surprise us. I'm sure all of us have experienced times when we've run into opposition from other Christians because of a difference of interpretation. And, of course, we've also seen how sharp and bitter divisions occur among Christians and churches when even well-meaning people interpret things differently. This is an "enemy" even today that is not to be taken lightly.

The important lesson for us in this episode is that in confronting every issue or course in life we need to be sensitive to the counsel and opinion of others, but at the same time we must find our guidance through the direction of the Holy Spirit. Frequently, this saves us from making hasty and wrong decisions.

Paul held steady in Tyre in the face of what seemed to be conflicting guidance because he *knew* he'd had positive guidance from God. And apparently, he was able to do this without offending his Christian friends who were immensely concerned for his safety. So often we Christians offend each other by the strident manner in which we air our "convictions." But if we've received the quiet assurance of God's Spirit, we can relax and follow gracefully.

Doubtless, you have had similar experiences, but I remember so well what happened to my family and me when we felt the Spirit was moving me away from being the pastor of a church to a position of teaching in a seminary. For more than two years we listened carefully as we felt God was talking to us about a change of vocation. Finally, when we announced our decision, certain of our Christian friends said they had a different word from the Lord—yes, I had a gift of teaching, but they believed I should use it in the local church. But this time we knew that our friends, out of love, were not rightly interpreting God's will for us.

This was the way it was with Paul in Tyre. God's repeated faithfulness and confirmation kept him from being shaken from the action that he knew was right. His guidance was not based on prejudice or on a hunch. He had positive word from the Lord, and that made it possible for him to rise above the problem of misinterpretation.

Paul's Visit at Caesarea.

After a tender leave-taking at Tyre, Paul and his companions moved just a short distance down the coast to Ptolemais where they spent a day with Christian friends (21:7), and from there they went on to Caesarea and stayed with Philip and his daughters. It was here that Paul had to face a different kind of an "enemy" or problem—*the problem of acceptance* (21:8–15).

After a few days they were visited by an Old Testament-like prophet from Jerusalem named Agabus. With the use of striking symbolism Agabus predicted what would happen to Paul if he went on to Jerusalem: "...he took Paul's girdle, and bound his own hands and feet, and said, Thus saith the Holy Ghost, So shall the Jews at Jerusalem bind the man that owneth this girdle, and shall deliver him into the hands of the Gentiles" (21:11). That was a positive verification of what Paul seemed to know would happen to him.

Immediately, Paul confronted opposition again, "And when we heard these things, both we, and they of that place, besought him not to go up to Jerusalem" (21:12). Luke, Paul's traveling companions, and the Christians in Caesarea begged him not to go on. But this opposition was not based on any kind of conflicting guidance. They didn't question his guidance from God. Instead, their opposition was based on a deep love for Paul and their desire not to see him suffer.

We see in this what a beautiful relationship Paul had with his friends and fellow Christians. He knew their motive, and he knew they were wrong because of the word he had received from God. But there is a tenderness in this scene that gives us a model for authentic Christian fellowship. Those Christians in Caesarea loved Paul and he loved them—he admitted they were breaking his heart by their anguish (21:13). But he held firm to his convictions and insisted that he must go on, and it was only then that his friends could say "The will of the Lord be done" (21:14).

As I think about this scene, I'm reminded of the confrontation between Jesus and Peter at Caesarea Philippi (Matt. 16:21–28). After Jesus had made a clear statement about His divine Sonship, He told His disciples that His relationship with the Father would lead to His eventual death in Jerusalem. Peter immediately spoke out with an emotional response, not based on whether or not Jesus was right, but Peter couldn't stand the thought of that happening, "Be it far from thee, Lord: this shall not be unto thee" (Matt. 16:22). And with that Jesus had to rebuke His friend.

Again, Paul and Luke and the others were on the move. They were taking the last steps on this eventful third missionary journey of Paul's—south and east they went to Jerusalem where "the brethren received us gladly" (21:15–17).

Blind Opposition (21:17–23:22)

We've all heard the saying, "Don't confuse me with the facts; my mind is already made up." At times this is more than a humorous aside; it becomes truth. And in this next part of our lesson we see a different kind of "enemy" that Paul had to face. Now the opposition came from his fellow Jews. And as we move along, we will see a demonstration of blind opposition that refuses to look at the evidence. Paul's actions and responses here are most insightful for us as we have occasion to meet similar people and situations in our own lives. As we have walked and sailed with Paul through these lessons, we've been impressed again and again with his courage. But now, as we trace Paul's actions during his arrest and imprisonment in Jerusalem, we are treated to an almost unparalleled exhibition of courage.

But back to his arrival in Jerusalem. Paul discovered then that a large number of converted Jews had received word that he, in his missionary journeys, was telling converts from Judaism to leave the Law of Moses behind (21:20–21). Even though this wasn't true, it was clear to the Christian elders that as long as these people believed this, Paul could have no influence over them. So they asked him to make a gesture of good faith by joining and even sponsoring four Jewish Christians in the rites of purification in the temple. It was felt that if he did this, it would prove his faithfulness as a Jew to the Law, and once and for all dispel the false rumors (21:23–26).

Admittedly, this is a difficult episode to understand. It raises a number of questions: Why hadn't the elders defended Paul and denied the rumors before he even arrived? By agreeing to do what they asked, why did Paul do something he didn't need to? Why didn't the Christian Jews show good faith and accept Paul's actions? These questions have plagued Bible students over the years. The Scripture itself doesn't provide us with complete answers to these questions, but as we reflect on Paul's words and actions throughout his ministry, we can make some likely proposals.

Throughout his travels, Paul had never asked gentile converts to first pledge allegiance to Jewish customs before he would consider them Christians. This was in keeping with the spirit of the Jerusalem Council (Acts 15). But what about Jewish converts? Here the issue was more complex. In general, we can say that Paul asked them to make a difference between dependency and repudiation. In coming to Christ they were no longer to depend on keeping the Law as their means of salvation. But they were not asked to repudiate their Jewish roots and customs. By complying with the suggestion of the elders and going through the rites of purification with the four other Christian Jews, Paul was trying to show that he had not completely broken with his Jewish heritage. And at the same time we know that he was not depending on those customs for his salvation.

How does this apply to us? That's a good question—an important one. I believe we have to cope with the same

The Beginning of Trouble in Jerusalem.

issue—distinguishing between dependency and repudiation. Often in the heat of post-conversion faith, we give the impression that repudiation of the past is the only way to find authentic Christianity. In doing this we may cause people out of our past to feel rejected because of a "better than you" attitude. It is terribly easy, especially for new Christians, to give the impression of feeling superior and spiritually exclusive and critical of anyone "outside the club." But if this is our attitude, we shouldn't be the least bit surprised if our witness is ignored.

This certainly isn't to say that there aren't things in our past that should be repudiated as we walk with the Lord, but to totally reject our past and the people in it is a mistake. Paul never did this and neither should we if we want to attract people to the joy and wholeness that comes from being a follower of Jesus Christ.

Then, too, cooperative gestures are necessary for Christians if we are to remain winsome and relational. "Holier-than-thou" types have never made good evangelists. If we are to avoid the automatic turnoff, we must continue to relate to and be congenial with those who have not yet made Christian commitments. Our line of demarcation is not the crowd, but Christ. But if we expect others to want what we have, it must be attractive and offer promise of a better life.

Paul is Arrested.
Unfortunately, though, Paul's act of good faith by complying to the wishes of the elders did not work out as planned. Instead, the opposition actually increased (21:27–22:22). While it is possible that most of the Christian Jews were satisfied, all the commotion attracted the attention of the large crowds that had poured into Jerusalem to celebrate Pentecost. And in those crowds were Jews from Asia, possibly from the synagogue in Ephesus, who knew about Paul and were violently opposed to his teaching. In addition to accusing him of turning people against the Law, they falsely charged him with taking a gentile, Trophimus, into the temple with him (21:28–29).

The rhetoric of Paul's detractors soon incited a mob spirit. In their bitterness and hatred they threw Paul out of the temple, slammed the doors behind him, and were "about to kill him." Luke then tells us that the uproar from the riot was so loud that it attracted the attention of the

Roman soldiers in the Fortress of Antonia nearby, and they came rushing out to calm things down (21:30–38).

These events caused Paul to shift to a second strategy in dealing with his opposition—*public testimony.*

As Paul was taken into custody, he made it clear who he was and asked to speak to the crowd (21:39–40). The chief captain, obviously surprised at Paul's knowledge of Greek and that he was from Tarsus, granted his request. And so, standing on the stairway of the fortress, Paul addressed the crowd in their own Hebrew language.

Paul's Public Witness.

In this magnificent speech (22:1–21) Paul explained the transformation that had taken place in his own life. But first, he clearly identified himself with Judaism, "I am...a Jew" (22:3). Then he goes on to give them details from his background, early training, and his early violent opposition to Christianity (22:1–5).

Next, Paul explains the cause of his amazing change—his encounter with Christ (22:6–11). Here he calmly rehearsed all that happened to him on the road to Damascus. It was a factual account of an event that happened—nothing to incite further the opposition of the crowd before him.

The final movements of Paul's speech (22:12–21) connect with Judaism in several ways—this is a reflection of Paul's diplomacy as he builds his case. His mention of Ananias in verse 12 was significant, for Paul described him as "a devout man according to the law, having a good report of all the Jews" who lived in Damascus. Then he referred to God as "the God of our fathers" (22:14), clearly implying that his new experience was rooted in and related to his Jewish faith. His entire speech up to this point had been a dispassionate witness of what God had done for him. He wanted them to hear his message so he avoided, as long as he could, language that would turn them off. But when he reached the place in the story where he had to say, "I will send thee far hence unto the Gentiles" (22:21), the crowd went wild, and they shouted, "Away with such a fellow from the earth: for it is not fit that he should live" (22:22).

What do we learn from this incident? I think most of all we learn that there may be times when we are called upon to express our beliefs and faith to people who disagree with us. But the model Paul has given us in this speech is very important—the spirit in which we do it is equally important. Witnessing to our faith should not be taken as an opportunity to drive a wedge, but to build a bridge. Naturally, our testimony doesn't conceal the truth, but it is to be reasonable and understandable and not given in a spirit of condemnation and censure—if we want to be effective.

Saved from the Frenzy of the Mob.

We see now in verses 22 and 23 the frenzy of the lynch mob in Jerusalem that day. The commander of the Roman garrison in the Antonia Fortress intervened and had Paul brought into the castle for interrogation. And as was the practice then, the questioning would be accompanied by scourging to insure getting the truth. It was a cruel practice in which a victim was bound and then whipped with leather strips to which were fastened pieces of bone or metal. It was against the law to use this flaggelum on a Roman citizen.

When Paul's attempt to vindicate himself by action and word failed, he moved to his third strategy—*official appeal* (22:25–29). He used his Roman citizenship to prevent a flogging. In my judgment he didn't do this because of a fear of death, but his mind was set on getting to Rome, and he didn't want to be disabled in any way.

When Paul informed the centurion that he was a Roman citizen (22:25), the soldier immediately reported this to his captain. Luke then tells us that when the chief captain had verified this fact, he "was afraid" (22:29) because the law had been broken when they tied Paul up. But then his next move was strange. For a reason that Luke doesn't clarify, the chief captain insisted that the Sanhedrin be called into session, and when they were together he "brought Paul down, and set him before them" (22:30). This was undoubtedly exactly what Paul was hoping for, and he eagerly seized the opportunity.

Paul's Defense Before the Sanhedrin.

Paul chose his opening words carefully to put himself on their level ("Men and brethren"), and asserted that his conscience was clear before God (23:1). With this bold statement the high priest ordered that he be struck in the mouth because of what was interpreted as blasphemy. Paul knew this humiliating act was uncalled for and even illegal under the circumstances, and he lashed back at the one who gave the order, "God shall smite thee, thou whited wall: for sittest thou to judge me after the law, and commandest me to be smitten contrary to the law" (23:2–3). Obviously, Paul was angry, but when it was called to his attention that the object of his verbal attack was the high priest, Paul apologized immediately, "I wist not, brethren, that he was the high priest: for it is written, Thou shalt not speak evil of the ruler of thy people" (23:5)—a quotation from Exodus 22:28.

There's a lesson for us in Paul's apology at this point. We, like Paul, must be willing to admit we're wrong at any time we exceed the bounds of Christian behavior. There's nothing belittling about an honest confession of failure. The wrong comes when we arrogantly refuse to make a wrong right and thereby compound a mistake.

Next, we see Paul as the master technician. He knew the Sanhedrin was made up of two conflicting groups—the Pharisees and the Sadducees—so he identifies himself as a Pharisee and the son of a Pharisee (23:6). This threw the council into an uproar because of the opposing positions of the two parties over the subject of the resurrection. At least some of Paul's fellow Pharisees were all for letting him go at this point, but the rest of the crowd created such an uproar that the Roman chief captain took him into custody again to save his life (23:7–10). In this scene Paul proved a point that both frustrated and infuriated his enemies—if they couldn't agree among themselves about the interpretation of the law, on what grounds could they accuse him of being unfaithful to it?

We also learn from this scene that there may be times when we, in faithfulness to our Christian witness, may need to use official appeal. Our stand against evil in any form may take us before both political and legal authorities, and when it does, we find a model in Paul of integrity and responsibility.

Luke now tells us that Paul's reward came as assurance from the Lord that his dream would come true, "Be of good cheer, Paul: for as thou hast testified of me in Jerusalem, so must thou bear witness also at Rome" (23:11). This was a promise Paul would have cause to lean upon many times in the months and years ahead.

But the plot against Paul thickens as Luke tells us how more than forty men banded together and swore to kill the

The Plot to Kill Paul.

Apostle, "We have bound ourselves under a great curse, that we will eat nothing until we have slain Paul" (23:12–15). This was not a threat to be taken lightly. The conspirators were deadly serious as they devised their plot.

Fortunately, though, through an undisclosed means, Paul's nephew heard about the plot and was able to get to his uncle and warn him. Paul, in turn, sent the young man to the chief captain where he exposed the details of the plot. Paul had recognized the seriousness of what was about to happen. He knew his life was in jeopardy, so he took the one course of action that was open to him—to seek *personal protection*. He knew there was no way he could protect himself, so he had his nephew act in his behalf (23:17–21).

Paul Escorted to Caesarea.   Now we get a vivid picture of just how dangerous this situation was. The chief captain to whom Paul's nephew reported had to be a seasoned Roman soldier with wide experience. He recognized the danger and took steps to move Paul out of Jerusalem to Caesarea, the seat of the Roman government in Palestine. But look at the precautions he took. The escort party was made up of 200 soldiers, 70 horsemen, and 200 spearmen—a total of 470 men. That's a lot of security to protect one prisoner! But this hardened soldier knew what he was up against, and he wasn't taking any chances. As soon as he composed his official letter to Governor Felix, the procession took off under cover of darkness, traveled the sixty miles to Caesarea, and the delivery of the prisoner was made successfully and without incident. Paul was now a prisoner in Herod's palace.

We see in this story that Paul knew his life was important—God had assured him of his worth even as He had assured him he would "bear witness also at Rome." Paul was willing to risk much for the sake of the gospel, but he never did it with the attitude that "my life doesn't matter." The whole point of this final drama is that his life *did* matter! And when it became clear that he was in danger, he took the necessary steps to protect himself.

From these experiences of Paul's we are reminded again that *we* are important to God. Our welfare and our lives are significant in His plan. While most of us don't face physical danger because of our faith, we are at times exposed to

It was in Caesarea that Paul was kept in custody for two years, and it was here that his three trials were held—before Felix, Festus, and Agrippa.

social, vocational, and even spiritual pressures that are crippling and possibly a serious threat to our emotional health. In such times of stress we can be certain that God cares. But at the same time we, like Paul, are to use all the means at our disposal to protect ourselves against those people and forces that seem determined to defeat us—this is fully consistent with Christian discipleship.

Expedient Neutrality (24, 25, 26)

An interesting and unique technique that at times enters into our relationships with other people is what is sometimes referred to as being "stonewalled" or "managed." This simply means that the opposition gives every appearance of being open and interested, but in reality that is nothing more than a cover-up because that openness is never acted upon. This is a terribly frustrating way to be treated, and it can frequently be recognized when the other person says such things as, "I hear you" or "We'll certainly look into that." But that's the end of it because nothing ever happens. This is what I call the way of expedient neutrality.

Chapters 24, 25, and 26 of Acts show this process at work in Paul's life. The time span for the events in these chapters is two years, probably A.D. 58 to 60. Paul remains in prison in Caesarea all of this time. During his incarceration he makes three dramatic appearances before the authorities. And each time we see that he is being stonewalled or managed—a victim of expedient neutrality. But Paul handles each of the three appearances with a forthrightness and decorum that underscores his genius and leaves with us a model for Christian action when we receive similar treatment.

Paul's Trial Before Governor Felix.

Paul's first trial opened just five days after his imprisonment at Caesarea. A contingent of the Jewish elders headed by Ananias, the high priest, traveled from Jerusalem to lay their charges against Paul before Felix, the Roman governor. The prosecuting attorney for the Jewish hierarchy was a glib lawyer named Tertullus who opened his arguments with a layer of flattery aimed at Felix that was calculated to make a favorable impression (24:1–4).

Before going ahead, though, let's look a little closer at Governor Felix. He succeeded Pilate as governor and was every bit as incompetent as his predecessor. It is likely he obtained his appointment simply because his brother was a good friend of Emperor Nero. His administration was marked by gross irregularities that were exceeded only by his infamous character. He had been married twice before marrying a Jewess named Drusilla, one of the daughters of

Ruins of the Roman Aquaduct in Caesarea.

King Agrippa I. Tacitus, the Roman historian, described Felix as "a master of cruelty and lust, who exercised the powers of a king in the spirit of a slave." Because of his disgraceful and incompetent administration Nero finally recalled him around A.D. 58.

It was this kind of a man before whom Paul appeared in his first trial, and as the events unfold now, we will see an example of *knowledgeable indifference* (24:1–27). After his fawning introduction, Tertullus spelled out the charges against Paul: 1) He was a pesty troublemaker; 2) he was the ringleader in the Nazarene sect; and, 3) he had defiled the temple (24:5–6). He then condemned Lysias, the chief captain, for taking Paul out of their custody "with great violence." The clever prosecutor built his case on false charges and half truths.

At a signal from the governor, Paul gave a brilliant response to the charges (24:10–21). It is not my purpose in this particular lesson to replay the fine points in detail of either the prosecutor's charges or Paul's defense because I want us to keep our attention focused on Governor Felix.

Perhaps the most intriguing thing Luke tells us about Felix is that he was apparently very familiar with "the Way"—a term for the Christian movement at that time (24:22). And now Paul had evidently made a strong impression on the governor because after Paul made his defense, Felix adjourned the court for a few days in order to give Lysias the opportunity to appear (24:22).

Some days after that, Felix, accompanied by his wife Drusilla, "sent for Paul, and heard him concerning the faith in Christ" (24:24). It may be that Felix wanted merely to show off his prisoner before his young wife. But Paul's witness to the power of the Christian gospel was so strong that Luke says "Felix trembled." Actually, the Greek word used here is much stronger and implies that the governor was struck with terror. This is understandable because Paul spoke of the need for righteousness and self-control and of the coming judgment. All of this apparently moved Felix deeply but not to the point that he was willing to accept Christ. In fact, Luke goes on to tell us that there were several such confrontations later, but apparently he felt the governor's sole purpose was in the hope that Paul would try to purchase his release (24:25–26). Instead, Paul was kept in prison for two years, and Felix comes down to us as an example of how a person can be knowledgeably indifferent.

We've all known, I'm sure, people who know (or think they know) just a little bit about Christianity—but not enough to have really experienced it. This kind of person is either hostile or, like Felix, indifferent. Either way, we, like Paul, are to be faithful to our witness in words and actions and leave the results to God.

The action in the Acts story picks up again. Felix is recalled and is replaced as governor by Porcius Festus. Among the unfinished business Festus inherited was the disposition of Paul's case. In a series of fast-moving verses (25:1–8), we find Paul making his second trial appearance before the authorities. Again the Jewish leaders leveled their old false charges against him. For two years they had been foiled in their efforts to get rid of Paul once and for all. Festus evidently saw that their case was weak, nevertheless, he was anxious to escape responsibility. He was basically a decent man, but he was anxious to win the favor of the Jewish religious leaders, so he asked Paul if he would be willing to be tried in Jerusalem (25:9). This was a clever dodge on the part of Festus, but Paul knew that to go to Jerusalem would mean certain death.

Paul's Trial Before Governor Festus.

In the case of Festus Paul was now having to cope with a different kind of "enemy"—*considered detachment*. It was obvious that Festus was trying to find an easy way out. If Paul had agreed to a Jerusalem trial, Festus would have been a sort of "figurehead judge"—a part of the scene, but not really, because they would be in the religious environment in Jerusalem. Paul, however, saw what was happening and made his formal appeal to Caesar. With this action, the future course was set. Paul would head for Rome and, no doubt, Festus was pleased because this took him out of the picture (25:10–12).

With Festus, we see what can happen when a person is well-intentioned but unwilling to become involved. Whenever someone says, "Do whatever you have to do; just leave me out of it," we are confronted by an "enemy" of detachment. When we really care about a person or situation, *we become involved*.

The final act in this drama brings Paul face-to-face with King Agrippa who, as we shall see, came to represent the "enemy" of *interested activity*. Agrippa was a relatively unimportant king who ruled over a small piece of Palestinian territory. He moves into the scene now along with his wife Bernice to pay his respects to the new Roman governor. Festus apparently knew that Agrippa was very familiar with the Jewish religion, so we find him explaining Paul's

Paul's Trial Before King Agrippa.

case to the visiting king (25:13–22). And next we learn that Agrippa was so interested that he said, "I would also hear the man myself." And now we move into one of the most interesting stories in the book of Acts.

Historical information would give us cause to believe that Agrippa's desire to hear Paul was based on more than just a fulfillment of duty. He was a grandson of King Herod, who had been told about the birth of Jesus by the wise men and had then ordered the murder of the male children in and around Bethlehem. His father, Agrippa I, had executed James and imprisoned Peter. The tragic death of Agrippa I is described in Acts 12:20–23. When Agrippa II appears on the scene, we could almost say that animosity for Christianity was in his genes. Nevertheless, he consented to hear Paul out (25:22), although we are not told why he wanted to get involved in the dispute. It is possible that Luke included the incident in such detail in order to make two points.

First, we can never predict how people will react to the gospel. If family line had been any indicator, Agrippa would have been placed on the "hopeless" list. It would have been impossible for him to have been reared in the Herodian environment without having heard the stories and seen the anger and hatred in both his father and grandfather. If ever there was a person predisposed to rejecting Christ, it was Agrippa. But as this scene clearly shows, Agrippa was both moved and intrigued by what he heard.

As a young student in his early twenties, Lew Wallace was fiercely opposed to Christianity. He and a friend determined to investigate the Christian phenomenon, especially the person of Christ, with the intent of producing a book that would discredit the whole affair. The story is now history. In the process of researching the person of Christ as portrayed in the Bible, Lew Wallace was converted. The resulting novel, *Ben Hur*, provided a positive view of Christ and Christianity, sold more than 300,000 copies in ten years, and as a work of literature helped to popularize the historical novel as an acceptable literary form. All of this was by one who started out determined to undermine the whole thing!

We must not be too quick to pigeonhole the "Agrippas" in our circle of acquaintances. Where they would seem to be headed may not be where they wind up. It might just be that Agrippa had heard so many bad things about Christianity that he decided there must be something to it or else his father and grandfather would not have spent so much time trying to stamp it out. Like Shakespeare's character who said, "Me thinkest thou protesteth too much," Agrippa may have sensed in his forebears an overreaction, at least to the extent that he wanted to check it out for himself. We learn from this that it is a mistake to write off anyone as a likely candidate for Christianity.

But the second point is equally important: interest alone is not enough to produce conversion. Agrippa certainly gave Paul an honest hearing as we see in Luke's lengthy account (26:2–29). Because this is one of the longest defenses recorded in Acts, we will look at it more closely in a moment. For now, it is useful because it shows that Agrippa was interested and even more by what Paul had to say.

We mustn't read more into the king's response to Paul than is intended. His words as we have them here, "Almost thou persuadest me to be a Christian" are not accurate in terms of the way we use English today. It implies that Paul came within a hair's breadth of converting the king. In actual fact, the king was moved, but not that much. The Greek term isn't easy to interpret, but I believe it allows this kind of an expanded translation of Agrippa's words, "I see what you're up to. You think that in these few words you can persuade me to become a Christian." In other words, Agrippa apparently saw that beyond the testimony was Paul's deeper evangelistic intention. And at that point, the king's background took over, quenching any interest that the testimony might have kindled.

In fairness to Agrippa, his assessment of the situation was accurate. Paul had done nothing to deserve death. And as far as we can tell, Agrippa found no fundamental fault with the gospel as Paul had presented it. But even interested inactivity on the king's part failed to change anything. Paul went on to Rome and Agrippa remained an unbeliever. For Agrippa the expedient thing to do was just to leave things as they were both for himself and for Paul.

Before leaving this lesson, though, we need to look more closely at Paul's testimony before Agrippa. In it we find several reminders of attitudes and approaches that can help us as we bear witness for our faith.

First and up front, we detect a note of *courtesy* (26:1–3).

Paul's Attitude During His Appearance Before King Agrippa.

In our witness for Christ, we must remember that no good can come from any other approach. Whenever we lose respect for another person's humanity and position, we have undermined the opportunity for fruitful interpersonal relations and Christian witness. I had a friend once who blew an opportunity for witnessing to a superior by saying, "I don't care who you are, you need to know Jesus." It's a mark of simple human decency to show respect to another person. Paul knew Agrippa's background, and he saw through the pompous front, but this did not erase the note of courtesy from the introduction to his witness.

Second, we cannot help but be moved by the *content* of Paul's witness. Through a mixture of biography and theology Paul sought to give the king enough to go on to make a personal decision about the faith. On this occasion, Paul began with himself and ended with Jesus—showing how Christ had led him to embrace an entirely new lifestyle. Basing his words in Agrippa's supposed authority, the Old Testament, Paul showed how Moses and the prophets would support his experience and testimony. But if Moses and the prophets were too far in the past, he offered himself as a living example of all they had said. This blend of information and experience should always characterize the content of our witness.

Third, Paul gave a clear *challenge*. We've already seen, even as Agrippa himself saw, that Paul's few words were intended to do more than report an experience. Their purpose was to lead Agrippa to a personal experience with Christ as well. The final words in Christian witnessing are not "and that's what happened," but rather "and that's what happened—*now what about you*?" Witnessing without an invitation to commitment is only part of the story.

Most of us are inspired at Christmastime as we participate in the joy of the season. The nativity scenes, the live Christmas trees, the singing of carols, all give expression to our traditional love and acceptance of the Christmas story. But the *story* of Christ is quite different from the *claim* of Christ. Most people accept the babe in the manger. It's the adult Christ who walks into the landscape of our lives that challenges us to a life-changing commitment. Paul knew that day as he stood before Agrippa, Bernice, and Festus that the mere telling of his story wasn't enough.

And so he urged them to share in his experience.

As we read the lines and between the lines of Luke's closing scene in this drama (26:30–32), we catch a hint as to just how profoundly impressed the Roman governor and the king and queen were with Paul. And I'm sure it wasn't just his words that got through to them, but also his calm attitude and demeanor. They were impressed!

As we have walked with Paul through this lesson, there has been much to learn. But Luke, in all that he has had to say, helps us, I believe, to face realistically the fact that we will confront "enemies" of all kinds and degrees in our Christian walk. But in the resurrection of Jesus Christ we receive the ultimate proof that "... greater is he that is in you, than he that is in the world" (1 John 4:4). This was the confidence that Paul had as he faced the various enemies in his life. And that is our confidence, too. Christ is risen! Christ is alive! Christ is with us!

Help me to develop resolute conviction like Paul, without being offensive, and let my convictions be based on Your Word. AMEN.

WHAT THIS SCRIPTURE MEANS TO ME—
Acts 21:1–26:32

Have you ever had trouble sharing your faith?

I know I have. When I was in high school, my youth group was given the opportunity to lead an entire evening worship service at our church. I had been asked to speak.

But what was I going to say? For weeks I poured through books—the Bible, some commentaries, works from famed theologians and ministers—looking for just the right ideas. More than once I started to write my comments, only to wad the paper into a ball and jam it in the wastebasket. I just couldn't seem to find what I was looking for.

One night while a friend and I were watching television, I expressed my frustration over not being able to arrive at a suitable approach for my talk at the up-coming Sunday evening service. Finally, during a commercial, my friend nodded at the T.V. set and said, "Don't worry about it. Just tell them what Rosie the waitress is saying."

"That God led me to a particular brand of paper towel?" I said with a note of disdain.

He laughed. "Course not. Just tell 'em, 'I tried it, and it works!'"

I tried it, and it works! Isn't that what Paul was saying in our Scripture lesson as he defended his faith before common citizens and kings alike? Even before noblemen like Festus and King Agrippa, Paul didn't pull out the heavy canons of theology, or rely on his years of scriptural training. He simply stood up and in his clearest voice told what God had done in his life—how God had appointed him to be a servant, and how He had carried this out.

All this time I had been looking in the language of religion for my witness. But Paul says God talks in our language. And that's how we can talk about God too.

Some of the most powerful witnessing I've ever heard comes from alcoholics who have kicked the bottle with the help of Alcoholics Anonymous. "I wasted thousands of dollars on booze, cost my company millions of dollars. I wrecked my marriage and nearly my own life. Until one day..." That's a witness that speaks because it's so personal. It's their life speaking.

And that's where we find the God we witness to—in our lives. Once, I needed to see a friend who was quite ill in the hospital. I'd been dreading it all week because I didn't know what I could say to him. And just as I feared, I had hardly stepped into his room when he asked me, "Why did God let this happen to me?"

I was searching for words, any words, when he began talking again. For 15 or 20 minutes, he didn't stop; he asked questions, made accusations, and wiped away an occasional tear. Then he paused, and just as I was opening my mouth he said, "I feel a lot better now. I think I understand a little more of how God is working in me. Thanks for helping me hear that."

Witnessing for Christ. It doesn't have to be a well-formed speech. Sometimes it isn't a speech at all. It just has to be you, letting God work and speak through you.

I think Dr. Norman Vincent Peale says it best. "I just tell what Jesus Christ has done for me. What more is there?"

LESSON 8
ACTS 27:1–28:31

Faithful to the End: Paul's Journey to Rome

Loving Lord, Thank You for Your faithfulness. AMEN.

In many of the devotional classics, life is described as a journey. Spiritual growth is seen as a pilgrimage in which we increasingly mature in the faith. In our journey, though, we frequently come up against unexpected events and trying circumstances that severely test our commitment. But faithfulness throughout the entire journey of life is the ultimate mark of a person devoted to Jesus Christ.

As we move now into the last lesson of this adventure-packed book of Acts, we follow closely in Paul's footsteps and observe his faithfulness as Luke takes us toward the end of the story.

Making It Through the Storm (27:1–44)

Paul had long dreamed of seeing Rome, of taking his witness for Christ to the Eternal City. Luke now prepares us for the fulfillment of that dream, "And when it was determined that we should sail into Italy, they delivered Paul and certain other prisoners unto one named Julius, a centurion of Augustus' band" (27:1). Three ships and more than 1,000 miles would be involved in this long and hard trip. And early in the journey Luke writes ominously the "winds were contrary" (27:4). This was true throughout

141

much of the trip. As we move ahead now through the events of this twenty-seventh chapter of Acts, we will discover helpful insights that can help us make it through the storms in our lives.

From Caesarea to Sidon—
an Experience in Friendship.

When the ship sailed north from Caesarea, Paul must have felt a tremendous thrill—even though he was a prisoner, he was accompanied by two of his closest friends and was headed for Rome. Luke, the "Beloved Physician" and writer of this story, was with him. And the second friend was Aristarchus, one of Paul's converts in Thessalonica. Both of these friends were long-time traveling companions of Paul. Mention is made of one or both of them in Colossians 4:10 and 4:14, in 2 Timothy 4:11, and in Philemon 24.

Frequently, God works through Christian friends in support and encouragement during difficult times. I'm sure we've all heard someone say, "If it hadn't been for

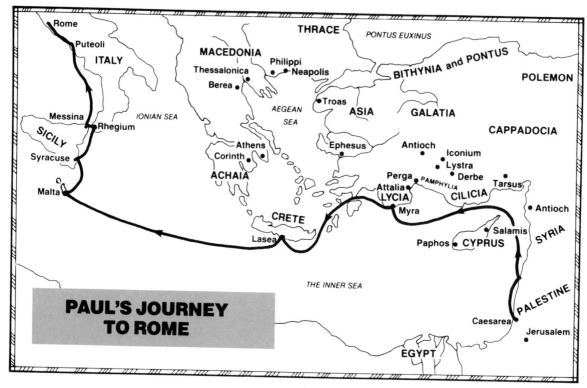

PAUL'S JOURNEY TO ROME

p;/

5/>

_____, I couldn't have made it." That's true! When our strength and faith are weak, we can draw on the strength and faith of others. Being a friend and having friends is important in the Christian community. I believe this is one of the reasons Jesus surrounded Himself with His disciples. And when He sent them out on a special mission, He arranged for them to travel in pairs. We draw support from each other.

Within a day or so the ship put into port at Sidon, just a short distance up the coast, and it was here we see that at times friendship can come from unexpected sources. Here Luke gives us a hint of what was undoubtedly the beginning of an unusual relationship when he writes, "Julius courteously entreated Paul, and gave him liberty to go unto his friends to refresh himself" (27:3). In other words, Julius treated Paul kindly and allowed him to leave the ship at Sidon and visit with some Christian friends there. Then, as we move along through the rest of this journey with Paul, we see a unique and friendly relationship develop between jailor and prisoner. Julius was respectful and courteous to the Apostle, and finally, when he turned Paul over to the authorities in Rome, he apparently arranged for a continuation of that same kind of treatment (28:16).

We never know where help and gestures of friendship may come from. I remember so well a time when my family and I were in the early stages of a long move across country. We had gone just about 100 miles when the lights on our trailer went out. In desperation we pulled into a roadside park at the edge of the highway. There was just no way we could go on into the night without rear lights. While we were standing around wondering what to do, a big eighteen-wheeler pulled in behind us. The driver climbed down from the cab and asked if we were having trouble. When I explained our situation, he got out his tools and in just a few minutes he had located the problem and corrected it. He then refused my offer of payment, climbed back up into his truck, and wheeled out onto the highway. Even now, although ten years have gone by, that event on the dark Texas highway stands out in my mind as an act of unexpected friendship.

Paul must have had the great gift of *being* a friend and of receiving the blessings of friendship. As Christians, we are to be known by our acts of love. There may well be times when being friendly is our strongest witness of Christ's presence in our lives.

From Sidon to Crete.   After leaving Sidon, the ship moved north following the contour of the coastline and then turned west between the island of Cyprus and the mainland of Asia Minor. It was here that they first encountered trouble "because the winds were contrary." But by staying close to the coastline they made headway against the west wind that prevailed at that time of the year and docked at the Lycian port city of Myra.

Myra was an important port of call for both Syrian and Alexandrian ships. And Luke tells us now that Paul and all of the prisoners were transferred to a grain ship from Alexandria that was headed for Italy. Then after leaving Myra, the ship moved on west against the wind for another 200 miles or so and put in at Cnidus on the far western tip of Asia Minor.

Because of the contrary winds, when they left Cnidus, instead of sailing due west to Italy, they cut south to Salmone on Crete and continued on the south side of the island to the port of The Fair Havens, which was near the town of Lasea (27:7–8). And it was here that we see how Paul used good *common sense* to help him confront another problem or "storm" in his life.

Luke drops a very significant statement in the ninth verse when he says, "...the fast was now already past." This is a reference to the Day of Atonement that was celebrated between late September and early October—in A.D. 59, the year of this trip, it fell on October 5th. It was a dangerous time of year to be traveling on the Mediterranean. Paul knew this from his earlier missionary journeys, and he urged them not to go on against the adverse weather conditions and warned that harm could well come to both the ship and passengers (27:9–10). But Paul's common sense did not prevail against the will of the centurion and the ship's captain who wanted to sail on west some sixty miles to the harbor at Phenice (Phoenix). They didn't take Paul's advice, but that didn't change the rightness of his judgment, as we shall see.

I recall so well one time when our son John was quite young and he got his hand caught in a fruit jar while trying to retrieve a small rubber ball. Naturally, when he closed his fist around the ball, he couldn't get his hand out. When he rushed into the kitchen crying for help, my wife calmed him down, told him to open his hand so he could pull it out, and then turned the jar upside down so the ball would roll out. What had seemed like an unsolvable problem to John was worked out simply by using a little common sense judgment.

I know, of course, that this childish story may seem simplistic when we think about the larger problems and complexities of life. But it helps to illustrate that God in His goodness has given us, as He gave to Paul, a great deal of good judgment and common sense that can lead us into experiences that are helpful in combating life's storms.

Before going on to the next part of the journey I want to comment on a point that I think is important, even though it's a bit obscure. When Paul warned the centurion and the ship's master against going on, he indicated that to do so would result in tragedy and loss of life. As we shall soon see, he was only partially correct. And so we can ask ourselves, "Does this mean that Paul, in this case, should not have relied on his judgment and common sense?" I don't think so. Rather, I think it illustrates the truth that as we move along at each stage of our life, we should "walk in the light that we have at that moment" and trust God for the results. We'll have an illustration of this happening in the next part of the story.

Caught in the Storm.

As the ship was preparing to leave The Fair Havens for their winter port of Phenice, the sailors were encouraged by the presence of a gentle south wind. With this good sign, they cast off, but shortly "...there arose against it a tempestuous wind, called Euroclydon." This wild northeast wind drove them out to sea and threatened to carry them clear across the Mediterranean to the Sytris banks, a notorious graveyard for ships, located off the coast of Africa west of Cyrene (27:13–26).

The crew and passengers were terrorized by the violence of the storm, and they gave up any hope of being saved (27:20). But now we see a calm Paul draw on the *resources of his faith* as he confronts this new crisis. And we see him, a prisoner, rise to the place of leadership. In the twelfth verse they had refused his advice, now they accepted it.

145

The crew had lightened the ship and trimmed the sail, but the ship still drifted on in the storm. In the midst of this seemingly hopeless situation, though, Paul gave them the good news that came to him from an angel of God who said, "Fear not, Paul; thou must be brought before Caesar: and, lo, God hath given thee all them that sail with thee. Wherefore, sirs, be of good cheer: for I believe God that it shall be even as it was told me" (27:23–25).

Paul's faith was rooted in a sure word from God. I am still greatly moved by the biography of Dietrich Bonhoeffer, the German Christian pastor who was imprisoned by Hitler for his faith. Despite the cruel conditions and feelings of hopelessness, Bonhoeffer's faith was an encouragement to his fellow prisoners. On the day of his execution he reminded them that the end of life here on earth is not the end of the story. His biographer writes that even the hardened Nazi guards were affected by his testimony of faith. When our confidence is fixed firmly in God's Word, we can "be of good cheer" irrespective of the turn of events.

I recall so well the experience of my friend Joy. She had been struck by cancer before I knew her and had enjoyed several years of cancer-free living. But then it attacked her again and spread rapidly through her entire body. This was my first experience of seeing just how fast disease can attack and destroy the body, and I was full of questions.

But Joy's faith was an inspiration to me. Through it all, and even until the last time I saw her alive, she was sharing with all of us a perspective that could only be had through a different set of eyes and ears—the eyes and ears of faith. But hers was not a faith that glossed over and ignored reality—it didn't pretend things were not as they were. Instead, it was a faith that said, "Even though things are getting worse, it's okay." I'll always remember Joy's gift to us of "It's okay."

This is the kind of faith that Paul had on that ship in the middle of the storm. And it is this kind of faith that can be ours as we draw on the resources of God in facing the storms in our lives.

A fourth element of making it through the storm is *simplicity*—getting rid of anything that isn't really important and getting down to the basics. The ship's crew had already started to do that in verses 18 and 19, but they redoubled their efforts as the storm intensified and continued to batter the ship. Now, in 27:27–44 this kind of simplicity is expressed in a further lightening of the ship and in doing those things that are a natural part of life— both were necessary for survival.

After fourteen days in the storm the sailors sensed they were near land. In all probability they heard the beating of the surf against the shore. They verified their proximity to shore by taking soundings, and since it was night they threw out four sea anchors and waited for daylight (27:27–29). When it got light, the presence of land was obvious, as was the fact that they were in grave danger of being thrown up on the rocks. Earlier, they had jettisoned the nonessentials—now went the essentials like the lifeboat and the cargo of grain. They were stripped down now to the bare essentials.

Paul's Fourth Shipwreck.

Simplicity is a popular virtue today. But what makes it more than just a fad is that it has been a way of life in authentic Christianity since the beginning. But still most of us wrestle with the problems of an "overloaded life"— over-burdened by demands and schedules and commitments. All of this overload seems necessary and important until we're confronted with a life-and-death crisis. Then we're willing to jettison the things that keep us too busy and the things we work so hard to acquire. At such moments it is only life that matters, not acquisitions.

Luke also tells us that while the crew was getting rid of everything they could in order to lighten the ship and make it easier to handle, Paul urged them to take care of such natural activities as eating. The storm had been so bad that apparently they hadn't eaten anything for fourteen days. Paul knew they would need their strength to meet the crisis of the next few hours. And as they ate, Paul spoke prophetically, assuring them of their safety (27:33–36).

Two things stand out in my mind as I think of this part of the story and relate it to Christian discipleship. First, we are to be faithful in the stewardship of things and time. We are to simplify life and avoid overloading of any kind. And, second, we are to be faithful in the stewardship of our bodies. On the ship that morning, Paul was intensely practical when he urged the crew and his fellow passengers to get the nourishment they needed for strength. And in facing the storms in our lives, proper stewardship of things and time and health will enable us to become better disciples of the Lord.

Now we move to the climax of this part of the story—the shipwreck itself. By now the crew and passengers had jettisoned everything possible and had eaten. After daylight they saw a bay and a beach and a creek, so they cut loose from the anchors, raised the sail, and headed for shore (27:39–40). But part way in they struck a hidden reef, and the ship began to break apart. Everybody was now on their own—some swam while others floated to shore on pieces of the ship, "And so it came to pass, that they escaped all safe to land" (27:44). This was Paul's fourth shipwreck—the climax to more than 600 miles of stormy nightmare from Lasea in Crete to the beach on Malta.

Miracles at Malta (28:1–10)

Neither Paul nor any of those with him on the ship knew where they were until they were on shore. But in this next part of our lesson (28:1–10) we get some interesting insights into how God can use the unexpected. In their trip from Caesarea to Rome they had not planned to stop at Malta. But this unplanned for and unexpected interruption became, for Paul, one of God's serendipities.

Paul's Snake Bite.

Let's pick up on the story of their Malta visit. The wet and cold shipwrecked victims were welcomed by the people of Malta. A fire was built to warm and dry them, but as Paul was adding wood to the fire a snake escaped the heat "and fastened on his hand." Seeing this, the superstitious islanders assumed Paul was being punished for some wrongdoing. But when he shook the snake off without any aftereffects, they then thought he was some kind of a god (28:3–6).

A Special Healing Ministry.

Next we read about Paul's introduction to Publius, the head man of the island who entertained Paul and his party for three days. During that time Paul healed Publius's sick father. And with that, Paul launched into a three month's ministry of healing that touched many of the islanders. And while Luke doesn't tell us, I don't believe it is too much of a stretch of the imagination to assume that Aristarchus, Luke, and Paul had many lively conversations and spiritual discussions during those months.

But the important thing to understand here is that this

unexpected, unplanned stop at Malta was used by God to exhibit His great power through Paul.

This reminds me again of just how careful we need to be in our attitude toward apparent interruptions. It is terribly easy to become so involved in the work of the church that we fail to see people and their needs. Reaching out to people in love and friendship can never be an interruption.

Leslie Weatherhead, the great British preacher, once told a story that puts life's interruptions and unexpected events in a divine perspective. He spoke of God as an Oriental rug weaver who sits on the backside of the rug pulling each thread through the fabric. The observer stands on the other side watching the process. To us, the observer, the rug-in-process appears to be a meaningless hodgepodge of threads and knots. Weatherhead then says that it is only when the process is completed that the weaver invites us to come and look at the finished process from His perspective. Now we can see the beauty of the pattern He has created.

This is certainly how life seems to us sometimes—filled with dangling threads and unexpected knots. But we can hope that none of the knots or threads of our lives are meaningless to God. Each thread has its purpose in the overall design. This seems to be the attitude Paul had during his days on Malta. He looked for and took advantage of the God-moments that occurred even in a place he never expected God to be.

There's another aspect to Weatherhead's weaver story that I like. It seems that when a thread unexpectedly "flaws" the carpet, the weaver skillfully integrates it into the overall design so that in the end it contributes to the final pattern. What a great word of hope for us! Even when something "flaws" our day or appears to "ruin" our intended plans, these may be beautifully integrated into the total fabric of our lives.

It is interesting to note that in Luke's final comments about the Malta visit he gives us a little twist by writing that the very people who started out being an interruption to the trip ended up by being the ones God used to supply the needs of the shipwrecked travelers. Luke says they "honoured us with many honours; and when we departed, they laded us with such things as were necessary"

The Payoff of an Unplanned Visit.

(28:10). "Faithfulness to the end" leads us to the place where we can recognize the presence and activity of God in even the unplanned places and events of our lives.

Ministry at Journey's End (28:11–31)

From Malta to the Italian Mainland.

The Rome-bound party headed by Julius, the Roman centurion, now boarded their third ship and headed north. From Malta they put in at Syracuse on the island of Sicily where they stayed three days, and from there they continued north to Rhegium on the southern tip of Italy. After leaving Rhegium they sailed north and west along the Italian coast to Puteoli on the bay of Naples where they were met by some Christian friends who invited them to spend a week with them. Apparently, this was acceptable to Julius, so arrangements were made.

It is in this concluding section of our lesson that we become aware of a number of parallel features that marked this part of Paul's journey, and which we need to incorporate into ours.

Paul Ministered to by Friends.

First, it was at Puteoli that Paul found a *supportive community*. Paul must have been greatly encouraged by meeting these people when he landed. We aren't told in Acts just how or when the Christian faith made its way to Italy and to Rome. But I'm sure the presence of these Christian brethren was a source of encouragement now to the Apostle.

And then Luke tells us that when they left Puteoli and headed north overland toward Rome, they were met on the Appian Way by a group of Roman Christians who had undoubtedly been alerted to Paul's progress, possibly by friends in Philippi. Reference is made in verse 15 to Three Taverns and the Market of Appius, which was located a little over forty miles southeast of Rome (28:14–15).

Again, Paul was ministered to by Christian friends. No matter where we go or how long we live we never outgrow our need for a supportive community of Christian friends. We are a part of a marvelous worldwide fellowship in which we give and receive strength to and from each other.

One of the great missionaries of this century, Dr. E.A. Seamands, was a dear friend of mine. Dr. Seamands went to India as a Methodist missionary in the early part of the twentieth century. In 1976 he was voted "Missionary of the Century" by the South India Annual Conference of the Methodist Church. He was a man of deep faith. After

It was on the Appian Way that Paul was met by Roman Christians and escorted into the Eternal City.

sixty-three years of missionary service, he continued to raise funds to build churches in India. He died there at the age of ninety-two while making one of his frequent trips back "home" to be with the people for whom he had given so much of his life. In ninety-two years, Dr. Seamands had not outgrown the need for community with his Christian friends.

Arrival in Rome.

In just a few words Luke tells about Paul being delivered to the authorities in Rome. I have to believe that quite a bond had been formed between Paul and Julius. They had been through a lot together from Caesarea to Rome. Although Paul was Julius' prisoner, he had been given deferential treatment throughout the trip. It would have been impossible for Julius to have spent all of that time with his prisoner without being deeply influenced. I think we catch a hint of this in Luke's description of the prisoner exchange in Rome, "And when we came to Rome, the centurion delivered the prisoners to the captain of the guard: *but Paul was suffered to dwell by himself with a soldier that kept him*" (28:16, italics mine). It would appear from this that while Paul was still a prisoner, he received special concessions. I can't help but wonder how much a recommendation from Julius had to do with that. Were some strings pulled in Paul's behalf? Could be.

Paul's Ministry As a Prisoner.

Next, we see in verses 17–28 that Paul was involved in *consistent activity.* His actions now are a replay of earlier episodes in his life and ministry. From Luke's chronology it would appear that just three days after his arrival in Rome he called the Jews together and explained what was behind his arrest and trip to Rome (28:17–22). And following that, at an agreed-upon time, Paul gave witness to the gospel of Christ, beginning with the Law and the prophets (28:23). As in the past, he received a mixed hearing; some believed and others resisted.

For us Paul is an unparalelled model of Christian faithfulness. He knew what his mission was and he stayed with it. For approximately thirty years he had been faithful to his calling. He presented Christ to all who would listen— Jews and gentiles; people of high and low estate. He had plenty of opportunity to be discouraged and even to despair. There were times when he may have been tempted to quit and go home, but he never did. His hardships are impossible for us to picture, "Of the Jews five times received I forty stripes save one. Thrice was I beaten with rods, once was I stoned, thrice I suffered shipwreck, a

Ruins of the once magnificent Roman Forum. Certain of the great buildings, such as the Arch of Titus in the distance, had not been erected until after Paul's death, but it was a center of interest in his time.

night and a day I have been in the deep; In journeyings often, in perils of waters, in perils of robbers, in perils by mine own countrymen, in perils by the heathen, in perils in the city, in perils in the wilderness, in perils in the sea, in perils among false brethren; In weariness and painfulness, in watchings often, in hunger and thirst, in fastings often, in cold and nakedness." So wrote Paul before this last trip of some of his experiences (2 Cor. 11:24–27). Yes, he was ever faithful through the testimony of consistent activity.

Throughout his life of service Paul's ministry is marked by a consistent strategy, a consistent content, and a consistent purpose. He was always faithful to his calling irrespective of the cost. And he carried this same spirit into his ministry in Rome.

We come now to the closing movement of our lesson and of our study of the book of Acts. It has been sheer drama from the beginning to this point. In these last two verses (28:30–31) Luke tells us all we know here of Paul's activity in Rome over a period of two years. This reminds me of the equally swift summary of Jesus' life and ministry in John 21:25. Sometimes I'm tempted to ask, "Why didn't the writers go ahead and tell us the rest of the story?" I could wish for more. But if I could ask John or Luke why they ended their books this way, they might well answer, "We've told you enough for you to see the purpose of what we've written, *and* enough for you to live out the implications of all that has happened." And when I look at it that way, I'm content.

We see in these closing verses a pattern of living that gives us an added understanding of Paul's faithfulness to the Lord—his was *a life well lived*. His was a life of openness and hospitality. He "received all that came unto him." He was obviously the kind of person others liked to be around. In that, he was much like Jesus. This is friendship evangelism at its best.

These verses also tell us that even though he was a prisoner Paul lived a life of courage. Our Scripture text says that he carried on his work "with all confidence." Other versions say that he carried on his work *boldly*. No doubt he continued to face opposition. But the fact that he was able to carry out his ministry with "no man forbidding him" seems to imply that even his opposition had respect for him.

And a third quality of his life that comes through in these verses is that Paul's actions and message were filled with content. He was busy "preaching the kingdom of God, and teaching those things which concern the Lord Jesus Christ." His hearers were given a vision of an abundant and eternal life, and they were shown the Person who made that kind of living possible. All of this was made real because it came from the experiences of Paul's own life.

The last thing we see about Paul here is that he was a

faithful communicator—he preached and taught. And what is equally important, his hearers *listened*. This means that the content of his message was not only good, but he was skilled in getting it across. By his life and his style, people were willing to listen.

I'm fearful that so much Christian witness today is not heard and received because of the lives and presentation of the "witnesses," many of whom seem unprepared and even angry. Also, we have a tendency at times to use a kind of "in" language that others don't understand. Neither Jesus nor Paul specialized in the use of religious jargon—instead their message was simple and straightforward.

While Luke doesn't tell us here, Paul was also busy as a communicator in writing during these days in Rome. Elsewhere we learn that it was during this time that he wrote his letters to the Ephesians, the Philippians, and the Colossians. These rich and powerful letters not only spoke to the Christians in those days but to Christians across the world for over 1,900 years.

With the completion of these last two verses, Luke stops. He has fulfilled his purpose in writing. In the first lesson Luke gave us what we've come to call the Great Commission—Christians are to witness for Christ in Jerusalem, in Judea, in Samaria, and to all the world. This was the story of Paul's life. For more than thirty years his witness had been clear. He gave it with friendliness and courage. The content of his witness was faithful to the claims of Jesus Christ, Saviour and Lord. And his witness—his teaching and preaching—was skillfully and carefully given. Luke has given us a thrilling drama of the establishing of the Christian Church and its movement out across the world. And he has given us a manual for effective witnessing and discipleship that we can use in our own lives.

Throughout each lesson I've seen Your love, care, and provision, despite overwhelming obstacles. You are my sufficient Lord. AMEN.

WHAT THIS SCRIPTURE MEANS TO ME—
Acts 27:1–28:30

They came in the 1840's to the new world, a small band of Dutchmen determined to find a place where they could worship God freely. A marshy swamp area became their home, and they named it Holland, after the land they had left behind.

Those early years were difficult even for such hardy pioneers, but in time the community began to grow. In time they established a school. Hope College it would be called; its symbol was the anchor, after the verse in Hebrews, "Which hope we have as an anchor of the soul, both sure and steadfast..."

I don't know if there was a Japinga in that first group that settled in Holland, Michigan. But my family has been in Holland and at Hope for a long time. Uncle Louie was all-conference in basketball more than 55 years ago, and my father works there now in the athletic department. I met my wife at Hope College, and it wouldn't surprise us a bit if our children decided to go there someday.

Perhaps it is my long association with the anchor symbol that makes this final section of Acts so meaningful to me. For in Paul's words I find anchors of hope which hold me steady when my life is threatened by violent winds of change and turbulent waves of trouble.

Anchors of hope. God provided them for Paul during that stressful journey. There were anchors of faith, courage, prayer, and an angelic assurance of safety. And those very same anchors will hold us steady in the life-storms we face in our complex world today.

Orville Kelley was a vital, hard-working man, living life to the fullest. Then one day he found out he had cancer. The doctors pronounced it terminal and said there was nothing that could be done. For months, Orville drifted aimlessly, buffeted by a storm he couldn't stop. Finally, in his desperation to save himself from being dashed against the rocks, Orville threw out his anchor. He prayed and asked God for the courage and faith to go on. His anchor held. And from that experience, Orville Kelley started "Make Today Count," an organization designed to help others find the way to overcome the storms of cancer and other illness.

Sometimes we find our own anchors of hope in unexpected ways and places. My father and I were driving home from a hockey game one March night through a late winter storm. The highway was snow-covered and the blowing snow made it nearly impossible to see. It would have been so easy to drift off the road and into trouble, but for one thing: the tiny reflector posts that line the road's edge. By using their dim image as our guide, we made it safely. Those reflector posts became our anchors of hope as we made our way home that night.

I return home to Holland as often as possible, and, inevitably, I find myself walking past the anchor in the center of the Hope College campus. And, frequently, I'm reminded of that hearty band of Dutch settlers who carved out an existence in those early days. But I also see in that anchor a symbol of what kept them going— they knew this story about Paul and that boat load of terrified men on the sea that dark and stormy night. Their anchors of faith and courage held them steady.

Anchors of hope...gripping the solid Rock. With them, we can go on as Paul did, "boldly and without hindrance."